Y0-BRT-009

The End of Protest

The End of Protest

How Free-Market Capitalism
Learned to Control Dissent

Alasdair Roberts

Cornell University Press

Ithaca and London

Cornell Selects, an imprint of Cornell University Press, provides a forum for advancing provocative ideas and fresh viewpoints through outstanding digital and print publications. Longer than an article and shorter than a book, titles published under this imprint explore a diverse range of topics in a clear and concise format—one designed to appeal to any reader. Cornell Selects publications continue the Press's long tradition of supporting high quality scholarship and sharing it with the wider community, promoting a culture of broad inquiry that is a vital aspect of the mission of Cornell University.

Copyright © 2013 by Cornell University

All rights reserved. Except for brief quotations in a review, this book, or parts thereof, must not be reproduced in any form without permission in writing from the publisher. For information, address Cornell University Press, Sage House, 512 East State Street, Ithaca, New York 14850.

First published 2013 by Cornell University Press
First printing, Cornell Paperbacks, 2016

Printed in the United States of America

Library of Congress Cataloging-in-Publication Data

Names: Roberts, Alasdair (Alasdair Scott), author.
Title: The end of protest : how free-market capitalism learned to control dissent / Alasdair Roberts.
Description: Ithaca : Cornell University Press, [2016] | Series: Cornell selects | Includes bibliographical references.
Identifiers: LCCN 2016027872 | ISBN 9781501707469 (pbk. : alk. paper)
Subjects: LCSH: Social control—United States—History. | Social control—Great Britain—History. | Protest movements—United States—History. | Protest movements—Great Britain—History. | Capitalism—United States—History. | Capitalism—Great Britain—History. | Free enterprise—Social aspects—United States. | Free enterprise—Social aspects—Great Britain. | Democracy—Economic aspects—United States. | Democracy— Economic aspects—Great Britain.
Classification: LCC HM661 .R63 2016 | DDC 303.3/30973—dc23
LC record available at https://lccn.loc.gov/2016027872

Cornell University Press strives to use environmentally responsible suppliers and materials to the fullest extent possible in the publishing of its books. Such materials include vegetable-based, low-VOC inks and acid-free papers that are recycled, totally chlorine-free, or partly composed of nonwood fibers. For further information, visit our website at www.cornellpress.cornell.edu.

Contents

The Quiet Crisis

It has been five years since the collapse of the investment bank Lehman Brothers—an event that triggered the most profound economic crisis to afflict the United States in a generation. Many other countries were affected as well, and some governments struggled to contain unrest. There were massive strikes, demonstrations, and riots. "It's kicking off everywhere," the BBC journalist Paul Mason observed in 2012. "The protest 'meme' . . . is sweeping the world."[1] But this was not really true in the United States: while there was unrest here too, it was not nearly as intense as in other countries. By and large, the United States had a quiet crisis. For some observers this was a puzzle. "Why don't Americans protest when they're pissed?" one American writer wondered. "Are people not angry enough? Not galvanized enough? Convinced that what they do won't make a bit of difference?"[2]

This was a reasonable question. Even if we did not look at other countries, and looked only at American history, we might have expected more unrest. Until very recently, it was an axiom of American politics that economic slumps were accompanied by strikes and protests that were difficult to control. Any American politician who practiced his craft in the nineteenth century, or in the first half of the twentieth century, took this for granted. Periodically, the economy would collapse. People would lose their jobs and savings, and then they would vent their anger in the streets. Politicians had to think carefully about how to respond to these recurring bouts of disorder. Should they simply put up with it? Should they crack down on protest, in the name of law and order? Or should they try to appease the angry public with new laws that made up for their losses?

Before 2008, the last great economic crisis to hit the United States was the recession of 1981–82. It lasted only sixteen months, but even then there was widespread unrest. There were more than four hundred major strikes across the United States during that recession. In September 1981, more than a quarter million angry people massed on the Washington Mall to protest the policies of the newly elected Reagan administration, and 100,000 people marched in protest in New York City. In the Midwest, federal officials were cautioned to stay "as calm as possible" as anger erupted over farm foreclosures.[3]

The economic crisis that began in September 2008 was longer and deeper than the recession of 1981–82. The proportion of the workforce that could not find work, or simply stopped looking for it, was higher. Many more families—almost 2 million between 2007 and 2011—slipped below the poverty line. A Federal Reserve study calculated that the average American family lost all of the wealth that it had accumulated in the previous decade. By 2011, according to the Gallup Poll, nine out of ten Americans were dissatisfied with the way the country was heading. This was a larger proportion than had ever been recorded before.

People were angry. And yet there was little unrest. There were only fifty-four work stoppages between 2009 and 2012—an eighth of what there had been during the shorter recession of 1981–82. "American workers didn't take to the streets," says labor writer

Stephen Franklin. "They took Pepto-Bismol instead."[4] There were some demonstrations in Washington, but none as large as the demonstrations of summer and fall 1981. There were expectations of massive protests at the G20 summit in Pittsburgh in 2009 and the G8 summit in Chicago in 2012, but these expectations did not materialize. There were demonstrations in Wisconsin against austerity measures, which many people thought would trigger a wave of protests elsewhere, but again this did not happen, even as state governments executed the most drastic cuts in spending since the Great Depression.[5]

In September 2011, the Occupy Wall Street camp was set up in Manhattan's Zuccotti Park. ("What took them so long?" Ralph Nader wondered.[6] He was not alone.) For a moment, it seemed as though Americans' pent-up frustrations would finally be released in a wave of protest. Within weeks there were similar camps in cities across the United States. The economist Jeffrey Sachs thought it was like 1968 all over again.[7] Others called Occupy Wall Street "the most important progressive movement since the civil rights marches."[8] As we shall see, however, these early judgments about the significance of the Occupy movement were exaggerated. By February 2012, Occupy Wall Street had been cleared out of American cities, and the movement was fading into history. "For all intents and purposes," *New York Times* columnist Joe Nocera wrote one year later, "The movement is dead."[9]

Many American progressives were mystified by the lack of protest as the economy collapsed. For thirty years, politicians in Washington had pursued policies that were designed to limit government and liberate market forces. This package of free-market policies, often known as neoliberalism, had been exported around the world. Now these policies appeared to be responsible for a spectacular and devastating crash. Problems of rising inequality and declining economic security had been exposed. Many other countries that had followed the United States on the neoliberal path had already experienced a virulent backlash against free-market excesses. But there was no comparable wave of unrest in the United States. "Economic inequality in America hasn't been this stark since the 1930s," the labor journalist Sam Pizzigati puzzled in 2013. "But back then Americans by the millions took to the streets in protest. Why aren't millions of Americans out protesting today?"[10]

The End of Protest

1

Schumpeter's Paradox

There is someone else who might have been surprised by our quiet crisis, if he had lived to see it: the economist Joseph Schumpeter. Schumpeter was an Austrian who immigrated to the United States in 1932. He was not, by any stretch of the imagination, a progressive. He hated Franklin Roosevelt and the New Deal. But Schumpeter also had a cold-eyed view of free-market capitalism. "Capitalist reality," Schumpeter wrote in 1942, "is first and last a process of change.... [It is a process] that incessantly revolutionizes the economic structure from within, incessantly destroying the old one, incessantly creating a new one. This process of creative destruction is the essential fact about capitalism."[11]

In the late 1990s, the revival of free-market capitalism that had been started by Reagan and Thatcher was reaching its high-water mark, and Schumpeter enjoyed a surprising comeback too. His idea of creative destruction seemed to capture the dynamism of the new global economy: crushing old practices, inventing powerful new technologies, and always surging forward. Schumpeter, the business magazine *Fast Company* said in 2001, was "the poster boy for the post-millennial, hyper speed, shock-a-minute economy."[12] But the vision of creative destruction that was popularized in the late 1990s was not Schumpeter's. It was bloodless and painless. It envisaged "incessant revolution" without suffering, anger, or resistance. Schumpeter's own view of creative destruction was much darker. Schumpeter admired the vitality of free-market capitalism but understood its capacity to cause anguish and resentment. "The history of capitalism," he said, "is studded with violent bursts and catastrophes." Wrenching change inevitably cloaked the "capitalist engine" with an "atmosphere of almost universal hostility . . . [which] increases, instead of diminishing, with every achievement of capitalist evolution."[13]

Schumpeter took this mounting hostility very seriously. He thought that it would eventually prove fatal to the free-market system. He was not quite right: in the aftermath of the Great Depression, laissez faire capitalism was wounded but not killed. Politicians in the United States and other countries were weary of the cycle of boom and bust, which was not just an economic phenomenon, but also an unending oscillation between social peace and social chaos. After the Second World War, they took steps to guarantee economic and social stability. For many years, these measures worked. They kept the peace. But they also entailed a substantial retreat from free-market ideals of the prewar era.

So here is the mystery that we want to solve today. Call it Schumpeter's Paradox. After 1980, politicians in the United States and the United Kingdom began to reverse many of the measures that had been set in place after the Great Depression. They wanted a return to free-market ideals. By the early 1990s, that free-market model was being adopted around the world. The result was a liberalized global economy of unprecedented scale and complexity. If Schumpeter was right, however, the return to laissez faire policies also meant unleashing the power of creative destruction. It threatened a return to that "atmosphere of almost universal hostility" about which Schumpeter had written in 1942, and which seemed most likely to boil over when the economy crashed, as it did in 2008.

Many advocates of free-market policies argued that Schumpeter's dark view of laissez faire capitalism was no longer relevant. The modern free-market economy, they insisted, was less prone to crashes, and generated such wealth that it was easy to compensate people whose lives were upended by market forces. But as the neoliberal model spread, experience showed that none of this was right. Many countries that followed free-market prescriptions after the United States and the United Kingdom *did* suffer debilitating unrest. This included many advanced economies that were struck by the financial crisis of 2008. In those countries, modern market forces were just as disruptive, and as likely to trigger unrest, as they had been in the United States and the United Kingdom a century ago. But disorder in the modern age was limited in the United States, and to a lesser degree in the United Kingdom, even after the crash 2008. In those two countries, the link between free-market economics and unrest seemed to have been broken. How did this happen?

There is an answer to this question, but we have to dig to find it. While technocrats in Washington and London were always been happy to provide other countries with detailed instructions on how to dismantle barriers to the operation of market forces, they were never so explicit about the methods that were used to manage the risk of unrest at home. Still, there was a formula. It has three important components. The first involved disabling the capacity to mobilize protest, mainly through measures that weakened the capacity of workers to organize. The second involved the reinvention of policing, to squash the new forms of networked protest that rose up as the power of organized labor declined. And the third involved ceding emergency powers to technocrats so that they could take steps to avoid full-blown economic calamities. In the two leading free-market nations, this was the unstated formula for keeping the peace. As we will see, there are important ways in which it contradicted our usual understanding of what the promarket reform program was all about. An economic program that aims at shrinking the role of government in general actually depended on making an important part of government (that is, domestic security forces) more robust than ever before. For police forces, in other words, this was the era of *big* government. Similarly, an economic program that was usually criticized for its doctrinal rigidity—that is, its unflinching attachment to cold principle—proved to be deeply pragmatic in moments of crisis. Experimentation in economic policy was allowed, so long as it was technocrats rather than politicians who did the experimenting.

In other ways, though, this formula for keeping the peace fit well with our preconceptions about what neoliberalism is about. It rested on an unprecedented intolerance for economic and social disruption and a deep skepticism about democratic politics. In fact, it threatened to extinguish crowd politics—that is, the method of expressing political and economic grievances through collective action in the streets. Citizens were told that they had a remedy through the traditional mechanisms of democratic politics. But this was not much of a consolation in an age when democratic institutions were crippled or captured by market forces.

2

Controlling Disorder in the First Liberal Age

There have been two great ages of free-market capitalism. The first spanned the nineteenth and early twentieth centuries, and came to a definite end after the Great Depression. The second age—marked by the revival of free-market principles that became known as neoliberalism—began with the election of British Prime Minister Margaret Thatcher in 1979 and President Ronald Reagan in 1980, and was a global phenomenon by the early 1990s.

These two ages were united by a faith in free markets and skepticism about government activism. But they were divided on a crucial question: Whether a market economy was inherently volatile, or inherently stable? As we will see later, the neoliberal age was distinguished by the belief that free markets were essentially self-stabilizing. It was commonly accepted that the market economy produced steady growth and adjusted smoothly to surprises. Moreover, the gains from growth were thought to be large enough that people whose lives were turned upside down because of economic transformations could be compensated easily for their suffering. As economists liked to say in the neoliberal age, a rising tide lifts all boats: eventually, *everyone* is better off in a free-market economy.

Few people living in the first age of liberalism had such a happy view of free-market capitalism. Schumpeter was not alone in recognizing that the system produced spectacular wealth, but also great pain, as market forces destroyed old ways of living. Karl Marx and Friedrich Engels, who witnessed the early stages of British industrialization, concluded in 1848 that capitalist development involved the "constant revolutionizing of production, uninterrupted disturbance of all social conditions, everlasting uncertainty, and agitation."[14] This was the demon that Schumpeter later called creative destruction.

Not only was free-market capitalism remorseless in destroying traditional ways of life. It was also temperamental and prone to wild swings in performance. As the British journalist Walter Bagehot noted in 1873, the power of the system was matched by its delicacy. Economic collapses happened so often that they were taken to be an inevitability, and the main question for economists was whether the timing of slumps could be predicted.[15] The invention of the roller coaster in 1885 was fortunate, because it provided a metaphor for the experience of everyday life: giddy highs followed by sickening plunges. "Boom and slump, slump and boom; such is all financial and commercial history," wrote *Everybody's Magazine* in 1904. "A panic every so many years; then recovery; then over-stimulation, and panic again. . . . Bury the dead, cart off the cripples!"[16]

Bread or Blood

But the dead were not really the problem. It was the living who caused all the trouble: workers who lost their jobs and savings, and households that could no longer afford food, housing, or clothes. When creative destruction took hold, people would organize massive marches and demonstrations. They would collect themselves into unions and go on strike. Sometimes they would vandalize factories and riot in city streets. Every significant economic collapse mutated into a crisis of public order. By the end of the nineteenth century, this mutation was accepted as an inevitability, just as economic collapse was regarded as an inevitability. Periodic bouts of popular unrest were intrinsic to the free-market system. The British, pioneers of laissez faire capitalism, learned this very quickly. Certainly, the early decades of the industrial revolution constituted a period of extraordinary material progress. Per capita consumption doubled between 1800 and 1850. Britons marveled at the advent of complex methods of factory production, the "annihilation of space and time" by railways, and the growth of foreign trade. In 1851, Britain's Royal Society of Arts hosted a Great Exhibition in London to celebrate the nation's progress. "The eyes ache, the brain reels," one American visitor wrote, "with this never ending succession of the sumptuous and the gorgeous; . . . this maze of sensual delights, of costly luxuries."[17] However, all of this was obtained at a price. The market economy that produced this bounty was also prone to manias and depressions. It destroyed traditional trades and patterns of life. It left the poor vulnerable to sudden swings in wages and food prices. It created industrial slums that were filthy and disease ridden. The capacity of the capitalist process to produce wealth was equaled by its ability to produce reasons for public outrage.

The British state struggled to contain this outrage. Manchester, a center of British manufacturing, quickly gained "an unenviable notoriety on account of its rioting propensities."[18] In 1808, the city experienced the first of a series of major strikes. Fifteen thousand weavers gathered to protest low wages. They were dispersed by soldiers. "I saw them fire," wrote a correspondent for the *Times* of London, "and observed several wounded wretches carried to the infirmary. . . . I have just seen a poor old man's widow, who is left with five children. Her husband was shot. . . . An apothecary has been sent to dress the wounds of many who were badly hurt by the swords and bayonets of the soldiery."[19]

The 1808 strike marked the beginning of a decade of intense unrest generated by the spread of the market economy. Across the English Midlands, workers began wrecking the new machinery that was destroying the price of their labor. The British government deployed twelve thousand troops to stop them—more than Duke of Wellington had taken to fight Napoleon in the Iberian Peninsula only two years earlier. Then spikes in the price of food caused another wave of rioting. "*Bread or blood!* was the motto," William Cobbett reported in 1816.[20] The following year, twenty-five thousand workers gathered in Manchester to begin a march to London, protesting conditions in the textile industry. Cavalry broke up the protest. There was an even larger demonstration of sixty thousand people in Manchester two years later. Cavalry charged the crowd, killing ten and injuring hundreds with their sabers.

Unrest swelled again at the end of the 1820s, when the British economy endured another slump. In November 1830, an unlucky crowd of protesters in central London made history when they experienced an innovation in riot control: a charge not by cavalry, but by truncheon-wielding officers of London's new Metropolitan Police.[21] Troubles continued over the next five years. Outside London these were dealt with in the conventional way. "For God's sake send out troops," appealed one member of Parliament, besieged by angry farmers in 1830, "Or we shall all be destroyed."[22] The British government also struggled to maintain peace in the early 1840s, as the economy entered another slump. In 1842, the Whig politician Lord Melbourne wrote to Queen Victoria that he viewed "tumults in the manufacturing districts with great alarm. . . . There is a great mass of discontented feeling in the country ... [arising] from the distress and destitution which will fall at times upon a great manufacturing population. ... [It] is certainly very near, if not actually a rebellion."[23] Authorities in London became preoccupied with the task of managing troop deployments across the country. "Pressure on the military force," writes the historian F. C. Mather, "was considerable."[24]

Eventually the British government hit on the doctrine of overwhelming force. In 1848 a movement of radical reformers who called themselves Chartists announced plans for a massive demonstration on Kennington Common, only a short march from Parliament. The contrast between the bright and dark aspects of the industrial revolution was starkly revealed. In another part of London, the Royal Society of Arts was preparing for the spectacular exhibition of 1851. Meanwhile the announcement of the Chartist demonstration provoked panic within the governing class. "An army of 170,000 in strength was hastily levied. ... All available troops were collected, and carefully massed at certain central points from which they could easily be brought to defend the bridges over the Thames, and watch the two miles of road that separated Kennington Common from Westminster Bridge."[25] With this extraordinary demonstration of state power—larger in number than the force marshaled by the United States to invade Iraq in 2003, and all crowded into a few square miles of central London—the Chartists' demonstration collapsed.

Throughout the first half of the nineteenth century, the United Kingdom established itself as the vanguard state of laissez faire capitalism. In the second half of the nineteenth century, this title was transferred to the United States. And there were strong commonalities between these two phases of the first liberal age. In the United States, as in the United Kingdom, laissez faire capitalism demonstrated its capacity to generate unprecedented wealth. Americans celebrated their progress just as the British had forty years earlier—by organizing the Columbian Exposition in Chicago in 1893. But the American economy was just as delicate as the British economy had been. It boomed immediately after the Civil War. However, a panic seized Wall Street in 1873 and the country slid into a six-year depression. There was a brief recovery until the onset of another depression in 1882–85. There was a third crash just as the Columbian Exposition opened in May 1893.

Every one of these slumps was accompanied by extraordinary unrest, just as there had been in Britain. In July 1877, railroad workers across the United States went on strike, seizing trains, tearing up tracks, and setting fire to railroad property. "The truth," said one journalist, "is [that] the whole country has been for some time ready for an explosion of some kind. . . . The hard times have pressed heavily on everybody, and want always breeds discontent and restlessness."[26] Still, the nation was shocked by the violence. With railroads immobilized, trade came to a halt. Governors who called out the state militia found that their troops were outnumbered, undisciplined, and often sympathetic to the strikers. By the end of July 1877, federal soldiers were being deployed to restore order.

A contemporary writer said that in some cities the strike took on "the aspect of war."[27] In Baltimore, militia tried to regain control of city streets by firing over the heads of protesters. "But this . . . only exasperated the rioters, and they opened fire on the troops. The latter now leveled their pieces and fired point-blank into the dense and yelling mass."[28] In Philadelphia, soldiers took refuge in a railroad roundhouse until rioters burned them out. Three soldiers were killed as the troops fled the city. In Chicago, meanwhile, "the wildest disorder prevailed." A mob of ten thousand men overwhelmed the Chicago police but were repulsed when federal cavalry—many of them "veteran Indian fighters, all bronzed and ragged"—charged through the city streets.[29] There was more violence when the economy declined in the mid-1880s. Hundreds of thousands of American workers went on strike in 1886 alone. In the Southwest, state militias were called out to restore service on the railroads. At a rally in Haymarket Square in Chicago in May 1886, a primitive bomb exploded, killing one policeman and injuring many others. In a panic, the police opened fire on the crowd. The country was seized with fears that the Haymarket bomb marked the beginning of an anarchist campaign of social revolution. Businessmen donated land to the War Department for a military camp on the outskirts of Chicago that would help to keep peace in the city.

Just as the Columbian Exposition prepared to open its doors in 1893, the American economy shuddered once again. State militia were called out to quell a strike at the Carnegie steel works in Homestead, Pennsylvania, in July 1892 and a railroad strike in Buffalo, New York, the following month. Kansas's populist governor called out state troops during a dispute with the Republican legislature in February 1993. Militias in five other states were used to contain a coal miners' strike in the spring of 1894. And state and federal troops disrupted a march to Washington by unemployed workers in early 1894.

There was yet another railroad strike in the summer of 1894. It began in Chicago, after the Pullman railcar company reduced wages sharply. Soon sympathy strikes paralyzed commerce across the country. The federal government ordered troops from its new military camp in Chicago to be deployed with machine guns throughout the city. The city erupted in violence. "Gatling guns and soldiers with loaded rifles scarcely kept the mob at bay," one newspaper reported, "and several times the troops were forced to charge with fixed bayonets."[30] Eleven died before order was restored.

The American economy continued this cycle of boom and bust, and peace and disorder, into the new years of the twentieth century. The economic turbulence that followed the financial panic of 1907 triggered a wave of violent strikes that lasted for several years. The main causes of the unrest, a federal commission concluded in 1916, were unemployment and frustration over the unjust distribution of wealth and income. The commission warned that these conditions could eventually lead to revolt by American workers.[31] The prognosis seemed to be vindicated by another surge of strikes in critical industries during the brief depression of 1920–21.

This unrest was dwarfed by what followed the Wall Street crash of 1929. By March 1930, the *New York Times* was already anguishing about rioting in major cities. A demonstration of 100,000 in Detroit that month was broken up by mounted police charges and "running buses and street cars through the mobs."[32] When President Herbert Hoover visited Cleveland to address the American Bankers' Association in October 1930, he was met by a parade demanding that he "do something for the unemployed." The *Times* reported that the parade "was dispersed by charging police on motorcycles and horses after a free-for-all-battle. . . . Women fell and were kicked and men were clubbed over the head until the police got the upper hand. . . . The police used tear gas bombs to disperse the demonstrators. At one point, motorcycle police released smoke clouds in the fumes from the exhaust pipes of their machines to rout a determined group."[33] As the Great Depression deepened, unrest intensified. In July 1932, federal troops marched with fixed bayonets down Pennsylvania Avenue to clear the capital of a protest by destitute veterans. They were backed by cavalry, machine gunners, and tanks—"the most extensive use of troops in the capital since the Civil War."[34]

Across the country, state and local officials struggled to maintain order as worker militancy grew. In Ohio in May 1934, National Guardsmen equipped with machine guns were called in to contain an autoworkers' strike. Two strikers were killed by gunfire. The National Guard was mobilized again—with machine guns, artillery, and "vomiting gas"—in San Francisco in July 1934. "It was a Gettysburg in the miniature," the *San Francisco Chronicle* reported. Later that month, Minnesota governor Floyd Olson declared martial law and called out troops to control a Minneapolis truckers' strike. Eight other states mobilized the National Guard in response to strikes by textile workers in September 1934. Martial law was declared in Georgia and Rhode Island and threatened in South Carolina. By the end of 1934, fear of social collapse blanketed the country.

"Can Capitalism Survive?"

Shortly before the crash of 1929, Joseph Schumpeter published a paper asking whether the "capitalistic system is stable in itself—that is to say, whether or not it would . . . show any tendency toward self-destruction from inherent economic causes."[35] At the time he had concluded that the free-market system was not inherently unstable. But Schumpeter followed the news closely. By 1934, he had emigrated from Austria and was in his second year of teaching at Harvard University. Events in the United States were alarming, and the news from Europe was worse. In 1935, Schumpeter began giving public lectures with the provocative title, "Can Capitalism Survive?" "No," Schumpeter told his American audiences, "it cannot." One reason was the inability of capitalists to manage unrest during slumps. "If, in the Middle Ages, something happened to displease the knights when their social function was threatened ... [then] they put on their armor, got on their horses, and galloped into revolting peasants as fast as it is possible. ... But capitalists can't do that ... and hence capitalism ... is an organization which can't stand on its own feet."[36]

Schumpeter was right to worry about the instability of the free-market system, and the disorder it routinely produced, but wrong about the ultimate consequences. Capitalism survived the Great Depression. Admittedly, the model of lightly regulated, laissez faire capitalism was beaten down in the years following the Second World War. But the core elements of the capitalist model were not extinguished. Embers of the old laissez faire model retained enough heat to ignite revival of free-market policies after 1980.

What error was made by Schumpeter and other free-market fatalists? They failed to see that British and American governments were gradually learning how to deal with the unrest that was triggered by the operation of a liberalized economy. In neither country did elected officials stand by passively as disorder filled the streets of major cities. Instead, they invented and refined techniques for containing disorder. Authorities in both countries were better at dealing with economic unrest in 1935 than they had been in 1835. Moreover, the process of learning was far from over in 1935, when Schumpeter predicted the end of capitalism. The Great Depression itself would produce innovations that improved governments' capacity to avoid and manage unrest.

There are four responses that might be adopted by governments that are confronted by economic unrest.[37] One response is to do nothing and tolerate the disruption. Another is repression, by deploying soldiers or police to contain and disperse protests. A third is containment, which we shall define to mean the redesign of law, urban space, and political language to inhibit the mobilization of unrest. And the fourth is appeasement, which involves a retreat from free-market principles to conciliate sections of the population that are likely to cause unrest. The four responses are not mutually exclusive. In theory, governments could combine the four elements—tolerance, repression, containment, appeasement—in many different ways. The combination actually chosen by government at a particular moment will be driven by political calculations: that is, what seems least likely to alienate powerful constituencies. It will also be driven by considerations of governmental capacity. To give a very simple illustration, the police force cannot be deployed to break up a demonstration if the police force does not exist.

Broadly, the history of the first liberal age can be viewed as a process of experimentation with each of these four types of response. For example, the earliest years of laissez faire capitalism were marked by a high tolerance for disorder. At the dawn of the nineteenth century, according to the historian E. P. Thompson, British authorities were sometimes reluctant to act firmly when poor laborers rioted over rising food prices. The cause of unrest was the advent of a market system that no longer provided workers with the assurance of food at a reasonable price. Some authorities balked at cracking down on these protests because they sympathized with the rioters' complaints about the harshness of the new market system, and because they calculated that less damage would done by rioters than by troops if they were called out. (Troops had to be used: there were no police at that time.) Authorities knew from experience that rioting was likely to be targeted against mills, granaries, and bakeries, and that it would not involve much more than property damage and the theft of grain and bread. But deployment of troops usually led to injuries and death.[38]

There was a similar tolerance of unrest in the early years of the American republic. The historian Paul Gilje has noted that popular disorder was often accepted as "part of the way society operated."[39] Everyone knew that unruly crowds had played an important part in the emergence of the republic. They had harassed the British colonial administration, often with the quiet support of propertied classes. Pauline Maier has agreed that immediately after the revolution, mob action came to be "accepted as a constant and even necessary part of free government."[40] And so mobs continued to enjoy some license, especially if they acted on widely shared grievances. For example, authorities responded mildly when a "riotous assemblage" gathered during a financial panic in New York City 1792. The mob was expressing a broadly felt frustration over financial abuses that had led to the panic.

However, tolerance for unrest began to dissipate in the early decades of the nineteenth century in Britain and the United States. There were probably several reasons for this shift. E. P. Thompson suggested that in Britain, the authorities' sympathy toward worker grievances hardened as free-market ideology took a firmer hold within the governing class. And as industrial centers grew larger, the character of unrest changed. Crowds became bigger, more diverse, and less disciplined. The informal connection between the unruly poor and governing elites, which had historically constrained the use of force, began to fray. A rising and anxious middle class worried more about preserving law and order.

Added to all of this was the reality that the expansion of the market economy was raising the cost of disruption in any one location. When patterns of trade were limited, unrest could be viewed as a strictly local problem. But unrest had larger implications when economies were linked tightly together. For example, holders of Pennsylvania bonds in London were alarmed when rioters occupied the streets of Philadelphia in 1844. If the government of Pennsylvania could not maintain civil order, they wondered, then how could it collect the taxes needed to repay its loans? The historian Karl Polanyi observed of the emerging market economy that it was

> more allergic to rioting than any other economic system we know. Tudor governments [in England] relied on riots to call attention to local complaints; a few ringleaders might be hanged, otherwise no harm was done. The rise of the financial market meant a complete break with such an attitude. . . . In the nineteenth century, breaches of the peace, if committed by armed crowds, were deemed an incipient rebellion and an acute danger to the state; stocks collapsed and there was no bottom in prices. A shooting affray in the streets of the metropolis might destroy a substantial part of the nominal national capital.[41]

The effect of market expansion on attitudes toward unrest was further illustrated during railroad strikes in the United States in the late nineteenth century. A disruption at one critical point of the railroad network quickly caused spasms throughout the entire system. An editorialist for *The Nation* wrote that the 1877 strikes were a "convulsion propagated through all the avenues of trade and industry."[42] Another contemporary writer said that the "whole internal trade of the Union" was suspended in a single day.[43] It was not surprising that federal troops were deployed so quickly. Trouble in one place now meant trouble everywhere.

Building the Capacity for Repression

When tolerance for unrest was exhausted, the next impulse of authorities was repression. This means the use of troops or police to break up protests and arrest ringleaders. But this is only possible if governments have troops or police available for the job. Today, we take for this for granted. We assume that any city or town of significance has a police force consisting of full-time officers who are properly trained and equipped. And we assume that the country as a whole has armed forces that are capable of quelling unrest without spilling an excessive amount of blood. At the start of the first liberal age, however, neither Britain nor the United States had security forces that were capable of managing unrest competently. The realities of free-market capitalism forced governments in both countries to acquire these capabilities.

Unlike the United States, Britain began its industrial revolution with a substantial advantage, from the point of view of the capacity to contain unrest. It had a massive army that was hardened by years of conflict on the European continent. In 1819, four years after the end of the Napoleonic Wars, there were still sixty thousand soldiers stationed on British soil.[44] As a result there was no doubt about the government's ultimate ability to contain unrest. But there was mounting revulsion at the results that followed when infantry and cavalry were used against unarmed civilians. This was why the British government established a professional police force for London in 1829. Initially, there had been widespread resistance to the idea of a permanent police force. It meant new taxes on property owners. For the British, it was also an alien concept that seemed more appropriate for continental autocracies like France. As a parliamentary committee said in 1822, a permanent police force threatened to extinguish "that perfect freedom of action" that was the birthright of every Briton. However, concerns about taxes and liberties gave way as unrest intensified.

Today we think that crime-fighting is the main job of an urban police force. But that is not why British police forces were first established. According to the historian Charles Reith, the creation of the London police force was "the direct consequence of the failure of the army" in checking mob disorder.[45] "The principal object of the police should be to repress disorder," one progressive legislator said in 1823, "the next, to detect crime."[46] It may seem strange now to regard the creation of a police force as a progressive reform. But for many people at the time, it was "an effective alternative to waiting helplessly until outrage and bloodshed justified retort in kind by volley-firing and sabre charges."[47] The innovation of a permanent police force spread across Britain during the depression of the early 1840s.

The new British police quickly developed new doctrines about managing large-scale disorders. An early illustration of this was the invention of the baton charge—a technique that is now familiar to police in many countries. (Police relied on it to break up anti-austerity protests in Rome and Madrid in the autumn of 2012.) The baton charge was the invention of Francis Place, a progressive reformer. After a skirmish between protesters and the new London Metropolitan Police in September 1830 that devolved into hand-to-hand fighting, Place advised a police superintendent

> not again to wait until his men were attacked . . . but when he saw a mob prepared to make an attack, to lead his men on and thrash those who composed the mob with their staves as long as any of them remained together . . . and that if this were done once or twice, there would be no more mobs. On the 9th November [1830] a large mob gathered in the City and sallied through Temple Bar, armed with pieces of wood. . . . My advice was followed. . . . This at once put an end to all rioting; no one was killed, no limb was broken, but many were bruised and many heads were broken; but there were no more mobs.[48]

The expansion of the free-market economy had a similar effect on the development of security forces in the United States. The country began the first liberal age with security capabilities that were extraordinarily limited by modern standards. In 1830 the U.S. Army comprised only six thousand men, responsible for 2 million square miles of territory. No American city had a professionalized police force. In moments of emergency, county sheriffs could call on citizens to form a posse to restore order. But citizens often refused to join a posse or abandoned it when confrontations became violent. State governments also maintained militias that could be used to restore order within the state. However state militias at that time were composed of citizens in part-time service who were poorly equipped and barely trained. An 1832 report for the Pennsylvania legislature complained about problems of "intemperance and riot" within the militia itself.[49]

Economic troubles compelled an overhaul of these arrangements that proceeded in two phases. The first began in the late 1830s and early 1840s. The United States suffered a severe financial crisis in the late 1830s that soon tipped the country into a sharp depression. The economic tumult produced disorder in major cities that proved difficult to contain. Martial law was declared in Philadelphia in 1844 after prolonged ethnic and racial conflict triggered by competition for employment. More than four thousand troops occupied the city after a bloody battle with rioters. There was no alternative to military rule because Philadelphia had no police force. Many Philadelphians had resisted the idea of emulating London's Metropolitan Police because they thought it represented a dangerous extension of state power, and an unwelcome imposition on their pocketbooks as well. But this was before the complete breakdown of civic order in the depths of the depression. Troops could not be encamped in the city indefinitely. In December 1844, Philadelphia mayor Peter McCall asked the state legislature to give his city a professional police force strong enough "to crush disorder in the bud."[50] The Philadelphia Police Department was created in 1848.

In fact, most of the major cities of the northeastern United States established police forces after the slump of 1837–44. New York City, which had suffered a massive riot over flour prices in 1837, acquired a police department in 1845. So long as the city was so sharply divided between "the rich and powerful . . . [and the] wretchedly poor," the *New York Tribune* editorialized in 1844, "there would be the necessity (as in London) of a civic army, a numerous municipal police."[51] Politicians in Baltimore, who followed the news from Philadelphia closely, also debated the need for a police force, which was finally established in 1853. City leaders in Boston were similarly moved. Boston suffered a massive riot in 1838 that was suppressed only after the mayor called out cavalry and eight hundred infantrymen. When news of the Philadelphia riots arrived in 1844, the president of Boston's city council urged the creation of a police force "strong enough to overawe those, who cannot govern themselves. . . . The tendency of events in our large cities has been such as must result in the creation of such a strong coercive power, as is not yet known among us."[52] The Boston Police Department was established in 1854.

A second phase in the development of American security forces occurred as a result of the violence triggered by depressions between 1873 and the late 1890s. The country was stunned by the ineffectiveness of state militias in controlling the railroad strikes of 1877. "Society is substantially unprotected in this country," *The Nation* complained a few days after the end of the strikes. "The country possesses no force adequate to the protection of life and property against a certain class of disorders which are liable to break out at any time." It called for the addition of twenty-five thousand federal troops, "judiciously distributed" to prevent future disruptions of rail traffic.[53] The secretary of war, George W. McCrary, agreed about the need for expansion of federal forces. "It must now be accepted as a fact," McCrary told Congress in 1877, "that Federal troops may be required not only for the protection of our frontiers, but also to preserve peace and order in our more populous interior. . . . Recent troubles have strikingly illustrated the value, in such an emergency, of the discipline, steadiness and coolness . . . which characterize only the trained and experienced soldiery."[54]

Federal soldiers were called on in more than three hundred labor disputes in the last quarter of the nineteenth century. But Congress resisted a substantial increase in the number of federal troops, and the burden of controlling unrest during economic downturns continued to fall mainly on state militia, by now more commonly known as the National Guard. The strikes of 1877 triggered a revival of interest in the improvement of state forces. "The necessity for a militia force in each state has been proved by the recent unfortunate outbreak of workingmen," the *New York Herald* stated in August 1877. "In all large populations there are elements of disorder which can only be kept under control by a strong repressive force."[55]

Between 1875 and 1880 the number of National Guardsman across the United States increased from 91,000 to 127,000.[56] States also reorganized their forces to improve discipline and centralize command, and prepared plans for rapid deployment to "important railroad and manufacturing centers."[57] "Riot drills" became a standard component of guard training. "We are now better prepared to put down a riot than ever before," an officer of the Connecticut Guard boasted in 1886. The *New Haven Register* described his preparations:

Suppose a mob congregated in any part of the city. There are men detailed as sharpshooters to pick off all persons on the roofs of houses or at windows who hurl down missiles on the heads of men who are marching in the middle of the street.... What the main body [of the Guard] will be called upon to do must depend upon the character of the mob. A Gatling gun at short range would, in a street filled with rioters, mow them down like grass before the scythe-blade, but the use of so terrible a weapon might not be required. The moral effect of a body of thoroughly disciplined men may be sufficient to disperse a crowd, the soldiers depending principally upon the bayonet.... There is no power like that of system, in which men have been thoroughly trained.[58]

The inspector general of the District of Columbia National Guard observed in 1896 that "states which twenty years ago had no organized militia worthy of the name, have by their own bitter experience or that of their neighbors, learned their lesson, and to-day have little armies in good fighting condition." This new capacity was used primarily to contain the unrest that flowed from economic turmoil. "Riots consequent upon labor troubles" were the most common reason for the deployment of state troops in the 1880s and 1890s.[59] However, politicians in the United States and Britain were also learning that having "little armies" was not enough.

Law, Urban Space, and the Language of Control

Critics sometimes said that nineteenth-century liberals wanted nothing more than a "night watchman's state." By this they meant a government so limited in responsibilities that it did little more than hire watchmen to light the gas lamps and call out the hours on city streets. But this was precisely the sort of government that the United States and Britain had in 1800, and which they had abandoned by 1900. A dynamic free-market economy required more than a few night watchmen. It needed police and soldiers who knew how to repress an angry crowd. The free market also needed more than this. Throughout the first liberal era, British and American governments took other steps that made it easier to discourage and contain unrest. They adopted more restrictive laws, overhauled urban planning, and changed the terms of political debate—all with the aim of preserving order as the market economy expanded.

The first of these three tasks was the development of a body of laws that would limit mass disturbances and legitimize the use of force against people who broke those laws. In the United Kingdom, for example, Parliament criminalized any attempt by workers to bargain collectively with their employers. This "anticombination" law was mainly aimed at weakening the negotiating position of workers but also limited their capacity to engage in mass action. This law was repealed in 1825, but businessmen quickly adapted by seeking prosecutions against union organizers for the common law offense of conspiracy in restraint of trade. With the aid of sympathetic judges, they obtained convictions for this offence for the next half century.

There were similar restrictions on worker organization in the United States. American courts imported the British common law on conspiracy in restraint of trade, and some states adopted anticombination laws as well. "The true prosperity of the country," an 1877 primer on American criminal law explained, "demands that all such combinations be, in some way, suppressed."[60] The depressions of 1873–96 produced a spate of common law conspiracy prosecutions against labor leaders, more state anticombination laws, and also new laws targeted specifically at interference with railroad, gas, and telephone companies. During the Red Scare that followed the First World War, many states also criminalized membership in organizations that advocated unlawful means to achieve political or economic change.

New laws did more than create barriers to organizing. They also set limits on the expression of disaffection through mass action. At the start of Britain's industrial revolution, there was already a prohibition on unlawful assembly, which was defined as a group of three or more people gathered to commit an illegal act. This ban on unlawful assembly was interpreted more expansively as the nineteenth century progressed. Eventually, even gatherings organized for a lawful purpose could be proscribed if they seemed likely to provoke *anyone*—even people not associated with the protesters—to threaten persons or property. In moments of deep crisis, laws restricting mass action were strengthened even further. In 1817 the British Parliament responded to a spasm of unrest by adopting the Seditious Meetings Act, which prohibited large gatherings "for the purpose of deliberating upon any public grievance" without the approval of a judge. Much of the law expired in 1824. In 1839, however, Parliament gave London's new police force the power to regulate meetings on public streets and make arrests for statements or behavior intended to provoke a breach of the peace.

A century later, in another period of economic tumult, British law was strengthened again. Police powers were used intensively to break up marches by unemployed workers during the winter of 1932–33, and London police imposed a ban on all meetings near offices that provided relief to the unemployed. In 1936 the British government adopted the Public Order Act, which increased penalties for breach of the peace and expanded the police authority to prohibit or limit protest marches. The law was adopted to stop marches by British Fascists, but was immediately recognized as a tool that could be used against the left as well as the right—as it was by the Conservative government of Margaret Thatcher a half century later.

There was a strong similarity between British and American law on mass action. American courts adopted the British doctrine on unlawful assembly, which by the early twentieth century had been consolidated in the criminal codes of most American states. In times of economic trouble, this law was ruthlessly applied. An important court case following the Haymarket riot of 1886 made it easier to obtain a conviction for unlawful assembly. New Jersey police used this charge aggressively to break up sympathy meetings for striking textile workers in 1924, and police forces across the country applied it with equal enthusiasm after the onset of the Great Depression, usually against organizers of industrial strikes, but also in other ways: to break up a demonstration of thirty-five thousand unemployed people in New York in 1930; against a meeting of distressed dairy farmers in rural New York State; against farmers attempting to block a foreclosure sale in Missouri; against students protesting about the comedy film *Red Salute*, which lampooned the American communist movement; and even against New Jersey theater lovers upset about the closing of Clifford Odet's play, *Waiting for Lefty*.

The United States also relied on other legal inheritances from Britain. American police could charge union leaders and protesters with breaching the peace, and often did. By the 1920s it was settled law that the charge could be laid if words were uttered during a public meeting that seemed *likely* to provoke unrest—even if no disturbance actually occurred. American municipalities also followed the British practice of requiring permits for public meetings and parades. A 1928 survey of major American police departments by the American Civil Liberties Union found that three-quarters of them had already established permit systems for meetings.

In theory, there was an important distinction between British and American law on meetings and parades. The jurist A. V. Dicey wrote in 1915 that it cannot be said that the British constitution "knows of such a thing as any specific right of public meeting."[61] At first glance, the situation was different in the United States, where federal and state constitutions recognized the rights of assembly and freedom of speech. However, this formal distinction had little effect on American law for many years. In 1897 the U.S. Supreme Court upheld a Boston municipal ordinance that flatly banned speeches on Boston Common without a permit. Bostonians, said Justice Edward Douglass White, only had the right to use public spaces according to such rules "as the legislature in its wisdom may have deemed proper to prescribe."[62] The Supreme Court retreated from this severe position in a 1939 case in which it struck down a broadly worded ordinance that Jersey City had used to block prolabor rallies. The court conceded that parks and streets served an important function as forums for public debate. Still, it confirmed that cities had the power to establish permit systems if they were properly designed. The right of assembly, it said, "must be exercised in subordination to the general comfort and convenience, and in consonance with peace and good order."[63] In the years following the Second World War, protesters and bureaucrats would argue whether the rules that bounded the right of assembly were correctly drawn, but there was no longer any doubt about the power of municipal officials to make and enforce such rules.

Like the law, urban space was also reconfigured to simplify the task of managing unrest. The most famous example of such restructuring is the redesign of Paris in the mid-nineteenth century under the guidance of George-Eugène Haussmann, a civic planner appointed to the task by Napoleon III. Before its reorganization, Paris was a city fit for insurrectionists. Its tangled and narrow streets were easily barricaded. It was difficult to move a mass of infantry, conduct cavalry charges, or obtain a clean line of fire for artillery. Haussmann said that he wanted to "tear open old Paris" by building broad thoroughfares that allowed efficient use of troops. At the time they were known as "antiriot streets." Haussmann added barracks to quarter troops at critical points in the city.[64]

Haussmann's work was not the first example of antiriot planning. Decades earlier, the British government began its own project of constructing barracks at the heart of each of its emerging industrial centers. Previously, troops had been barracked mainly in coastal towns. But circumstances changed, as Prime Minister William Pitt told Parliament. "A spirit had appeared in some of the manufacturing towns which made it necessary that troops should be kept near them."[65] In metropolitan London, a program of street redesign similar to the later Parisian project also simplified policing. Napoleon III told Haussmann to look at London as a model for his Paris reforms.[66]

European states were not alone in their efforts to reorganize public space so that it could be controlled more easily. American civic leaders undertook the same task in the years following the Civil War. "The topography of cities plays an important part in connection with riots," the Parks Commissioner of New York City, Egbert Viele, a retired general of the Union Army, told a military conference in 1883. "[The National Guard] should take the plans of cities. . . . They should locate certain places where the reserves of the military force should be, [and] determine upon certain buildings that might possibly be attacked, and look to their protection first."[67] Civic leaders took General Viele's advice to heart. Hundreds of heavily fortified armories were built in the centers of American cities in response to the economic upheavals of the late nineteenth century. A good example was New York City's Twelfth

Regiment Armory, completed in 1886. The armory was praised for its "solid fortress-like character. . . . At each street corner are flanking towers, with loop-holes and arrangements for howitzers, or Gatling guns, at the top. Around the entire roof is a paved promenade, protected by a parapet with many loop-holes, constituting a valuable defensive position." The heavy style served an important symbolic purpose as well. An admirer said the building was "a tower of strength of lovers of civic order and peace who remember the possibilities . . . of riot and disturbance."[68]

Boston's new armory was even more impressive. Financed by local businessmen, it was built in the style of a medieval castle dominated by a tower six stories high. Its walls were two feet thick and its windows were shielded by musket-proof steel shutters. The drill hall was protected by a draw bridge, heavy iron gates, and towers that allowed militiamen to sweep the exterior with flanking fire. The location of the new armory was "strategically advantageous because of [its] central situation in relation to the population, to public buildings and to the termini of railroads of the City."[69] Signalmen in the tower could communicate with the State House almost a mile away.

Politicians in the United States and Britain were not just reconfiguring the law and urban space so that it would be easier to keep the peace in hard times. They also renovated the language of politics. Politicians and businessmen who wanted to contain unrest quickly learned that the use of force had to be justified. Words had to be found to explain why soldiers and policemen were deployed against civilians, why shots were sometimes fired, and why protesters were arrested. A style of argument had to be invented to defend the new repressive capacities of government. One result was the popularization of the concept of law and order. The term was used with increasing frequency throughout the first liberal age, especially during moments of economic distress. When unrest struck the state of Rhode Island during the depression of the 1840s, a new Law and Order Party won control of every significant office in the state. The depressions of the later nineteenth century saw the creation of law and order associations in major American cities to promote "the enforcement of law against conduct detrimental to personal liberty, industrial stability and progress."[70] And the depression of the 1930s spurred the creation of law and order leagues that were organized to counter "the fires of disorder, violence and discontent" in strike-bound cities.[71]

Law and order was a rallying cry for conservative forces in times of economic hardship. It was more than just a phrase. It was a way of thinking that justified the use of force. People who talked about law and order believed that the threat to social order was immediate and severe. The alternative to repression was anarchy: "The destruction of all government, [and] the dissolution of all bonds by which society is held together."[72] And they did not see any tension between the use of force and the preservation of individual liberties. On the contrary, repression was regarded as the prerequisite for freedom. "Without Law and Order there can be no real liberty," a Minnesota businessman explained in 1920, "because there can be no security."[73]

Moreover, the threat to order was regarded as something that was alien to society itself. The real reason for the unrest of late nineteenth century, U.S. general Albert Ordway argued in 1891, was that the country "has been overrun by hundreds of thousands of the most criminal and ignorant classes of Europe, who can neither assimilate with our people nor appreciate or understand the meaning of our institutions."[74] In 1894, a government inquiry explained unrest in Chicago as the work of "hoodlums, women, a low class of foreigners, and recruits from the criminal classes."[75] If disturbers of the peace were not themselves foreigners, they might still be contaminated by "alien philosophies" such as anarchism or communism. All of this made the deployment of force defensible. In a sense, it was not a matter of preserving *internal* order at all. Instead, it was the traditional problem of defending society from external assaults.

Another shift in the language of politics also made it easier to use force. This was a change in thinking about the nature of crowds themselves. At the start of the nineteenth century there were still many people who took a favorable, and even romantic, view about the role of crowds in politics. Crowds had played an important role in triggering the American Revolution, acting with intelligence in the pursuit of democracy and liberty. And they had played a similar role in Europe. In 1837 the historian Thomas Carlyle commended the mobs that launched the French revolution: "So clear-sighted, inventive, [and] prompt to seize the moment . . . a genuine outburst of Nature."[76]

This was a generous view of crowds. By the end of the nineteenth century it would be displaced entirely by another view, in which crowds were irrational, unpredictable, and dangerous. One of the first writers to encourage this shift was the journalist Charles Mackay, whose book, *Memoirs of Extraordinary Popular Delusions*, was published in London in 1841. Mackay presented his book as a work of history, documenting the moments in which "whole communities suddenly fix their minds upon one object, and go mad in its pursuit." It ranged from medieval witch hunts to the Dutch tulip mania of the seventeenth century. Mackay extracted one lesson: "Men . . . go mad in herds; while they recover their senses slowly, and one by one."[77] Mackay's readers understood that he was not just writing about history. Notices about the new book appeared in the London press next to reports about "social derangements" in England during the depression of the early 1840s.[78] Its first review appeared in the fashionable *Court Gazette* in April 1842, which immediately noted that "our own day seems to have only increased our capacity" for popular delusions.[79] In later writing, Mackay said what he thought of the Chartists, a reform movement that was reaching the peak of its power in the 1840s: "A formidable nuisance, now happily extinct."[80] Mackay even wrote poetry that evoked the image of the crowd as a careless, credulous, and dangerous mass.

As the first liberal age rolled on, this pessimistic view of crowds acquired a more impressive pedigree. In France, political convulsions caused a reappraisal of the Revolution of 1789 and its consequences. The historian Hippolyte Taine, writing in Paris at the time of the Commune of 1871, refused to accept Carlyle's happy view of the French mob. The revolutionary crowd, Taine said, was "a formidable power, undefined and destructive, on which no one has any hold."[81] A few years later another French academic, Gabriele Tarde, concurred. "A mob is a strange phenomenon," Tarde wrote. "It is a gathering of heterogeneous elements, unknown to one another; but as soon as a spark of passion . . . electrifies this confused mass, there takes place a sort of sudden cohesion, a spontaneous generation. This incoherence becomes cohesion, this noise becomes a voice, and these thousands of men crowded together soon form but a single animal, a wild beast without a name."[82]

In the United States, the Harvard-trained psychologist Boris Sidis also presented the irrationality of crowds as matter of scientifically established fact. Men are highly suggestible, Sidis argued in an 1898 book, especially when they are lost in a mass. "We do not in the least suspect that the awful, destructive, automatic spirit of the mob moves in the bosom of the peaceful crowd," Sidis wrote.[83] But he insisted that the potential for chaos was always present when a crowd gathered. Sidis's book was a best seller in the United States. So was Gustave Le Bon's book *The Crowd*, after it was translated from French to English in 1897. Like Sidis, Le Bon said that individuals in a crowd lost their capacity to think clearly. Crowds were more primitive, with characteristics "such as impulsiveness, irritability, incapacity to reason, the absence of judgment . . . which are almost always observed in beings belonging to inferior forms of evolution—in women, savages, and children, for instance."[84] One American writer used Le Bon's theory to explain a march on Washington by unemployed workers during the depression of the early 1890s. A sensible individual "would have laughed at such a method of accomplishing reform. But the judgment of each was swallowed up in the impulse of the many."[85]

Le Bon predicted that the twentieth century would be the "era of crowds." He was wrong. The idea of a crowd as a distinctive political actor—as a thing separate from the individuals who comprised it, capable of exerting a powerful influence over the course of politics, and worthy of study on its own account, just as we might study presidents or legislatures or political parties—was dying. Throughout the first liberal age, governments had been perfecting their capacity to contain and repress crowds. They had better police and military forces, more restrictive laws, and better control of urban space. And with works like Le Bon's, they had better arguments for wielding their newfound powers.

Reducing Economic Risks

By 1934, the United States and Britain were at a turning point, so far as their strategies for managing unrest were concerned. Both countries were decades past the point where simple toleration of unrest was an acceptable policy. Each had developed more sophisticated techniques for containing and repressing unrest. But the tactics of containment and repression were still insufficient to maintain social peace. The threat to the stability of the American and British political systems during the Great Depression was clear. Democracy, wrote the political scientist William B. Munro, had "its back to the wall."[86] Could anything more be done to keep the peace?

Karl Polanyi thought so. Polanyi, like Schumpeter, was an economic historian. He was also Austrian, born in Vienna in 1886, three years after Schumpeter. Polanyi immigrated to Britain in 1933 and then to the United States in 1940. While Schumpeter toiled on *Capitalism, Socialism, and Democracy* (the book that introduced creative destruction) in Cambridge, Massachusetts, Polanyi was only a few hours away, at Bennington College in Vermont. Polanyi was preparing his own great work: *The Great Transformation*, which was published only fourteen months after Schumpeter's. In that book, Polanyi shared Schumpeter's skepticism about the durability of the laissez faire system. The rise of a market economy, Polanyi said, meant the "liquidation" of old forms of social organization. Misery and degradation were the ugly by-products of laissez faire development, and they produced intense public resentment against the free-market system. Left unchecked, Polanyi concluded, "the self-regulating market system would inevitably have destroyed society"—and thus also itself.[87]

Polanyi was deeply interested in the mechanisms by which societies protected themselves against the worst effects of free-market capitalism. In Britain, Polanyi argued, laissez faire policies had triggered a "protective countermovement"—a broad defensive reaction by workers, farmers, and other groups that suffered most severely from the expansion of the market system. This was not a unified or ideologically coherent campaign against liberal orthodoxy. Rather, it was composed of a number of disparate and pragmatic initiatives to control market excesses. Polanyi described the early accomplishments of this countermovement. By the end of the nineteenth century, British governments had established stricter rules on working hours, workplace safety, and child labor. They had adopted food safety laws and other public health measures, and reformed municipal administration to improve the conditions of urban life. Legal barriers to the organization of trade unions were also removed. Voting rights were extended, and Parliament was reformed to improve the representation of new industrial centers like Manchester.

Diehard proponents of the free market condemned many of these measures. "The more numerous governmental interventions become," the free-market theorist Herbert Spencer complained in 1884, "the more loud and perpetual the demands for intervention. . . . Every candidate for Parliament is prompted to propose or support some new piece of *ad captandum* legislation."[88] In Polanyi's view, however, these interventions had helped to preserve the essential elements of the market system. The alternative was social and political collapse. Polanyi had a name for his theory about the evolution of the British economy in the nineteenth century. He called it the "thesis of the double movement." The thesis had an alluring sense of inevitability about it. A movement to one extreme (that is, market utopianism) automatically generated a protective countermovement, which restored social harmony. In a sense, Polanyi had replaced the idea of a self-regulating market with that of a self-regulating society.

The double movement also operated in the United States during the first liberal age, but in a more limited way. By the eve of the First World War, American government had bolstered its power to control abuses in the workplace and marketplace. It also assumed responsibility for managing financial crises by establishing the Federal Reserve, a new national central bank. There were also political reforms, such as the introduction of direct election of senators, that were supposed to limit corporate influence on government. But there were some things that did not change despite public outrage. The United States stayed on the gold standard, even though this limited the country's ability to recover from deep depressions. The nation was also slow to follow Europe in establishing insurance programs to protect disabled workers, the unemployed, and the aged. And American law remained hostile to the idea that workers should be allowed to negotiate collectively with their employers.

In the 1920s, the power of the countermovement was even less certain. In the United States, fears about the rise of communism encouraged a crackdown on leftist activism and labor organizing. A succession of Republican presidents—Harding, Coolidge, Hoover—promised to reduce government spending and end "unnecessary interference with business."[89] And at the end of the 1920s, Europe and the United States were booming again, with the result that there was little interest in further government intervention. The boom "drowned all concern for the soundness of the market system," Polanyi wrote. "Capitalism was proclaimed restored."[90] Of course, the situation changed dramatically after the Wall Street crash of 1929. The Great Depression was a critical test for Polanyi's thesis of the double movement. If the countermovement could not win concessions at this dark moment, then perhaps it no longer operated at all.

In fact, Polanyi's thesis did seem to be validated by the experience of the Great Depression. The project of crafting concessions to critics of the market system was slow moving and still underway when Polanyi published *The Great Transformation* in 1944.

But the great theme of this project was already clear. It consisted of a massive effort to protect individuals from the uncertainties and dislocations that typified the operation of a free-market economy. Even before the Great Depression, British and American governments had shouldered some responsibility for reducing the risk of injury or death because of unsafe workplaces or adulterated foods and medicines. They had also begun piecemeal programs to support injured workers, widows, the unemployed, and the elderly. As a result of the Great Depression, these programs were extended and justified more coherently. The Beveridge Report of 1942, a document that would become the keystone of British social policy in the postwar era, explained the ambition concisely. The aim of government policy should be the achievement of "freedom of want" through an "all-embracing . . . scheme of social insurance against interruption and destruction of earning power."[91] A similar study produced by the Roosevelt White House in January 1943—the "American Beveridge Report," as the U.S. press called it—echoed the sentiment. The American system of social insurance that evolved in the postwar period differed in important respects from the British system. It was more uneven in its treatment of different kinds of workers, and relied more heavily on incentives to private employers to provide benefits such as health insurance and pensions. Still, the broad aim of policy in the United States was comparable to the aim of policy in Britain. As Franklin Roosevelt said in 1943, the goal was "to give assurance for all our people against common economic hazards."[92]

The project of economic reform went far beyond social insurance programs. The financial sectors of advanced economies were also rebuilt to prevent further cycles of boom and slump. In part, this meant reducing financial interconnections between the advanced economies. International finance was now regarded as a dangerous beast, temperamental and predatory, that could only be tamed by severe restrictions on the flow of capital across national borders. The reputation of domestic finance was not much better. In the United States, new laws were adopted to curtail risk-taking by banks and compensate depositors for their losses when banks failed.

Governments went even further in their effort to protect citizens from the volatility of the free market. Heavily influenced by economists such as John Maynard Keynes, politicians in the United States and Britain became more confident about their ability to use monetary and fiscal policy to control the behavior of the overall economy. Both nations moved away from the traditional gold standard. This decision gave the two countries' central banks—the Federal Reserve and the Bank of England—more discretion to adopt policies that would protect citizens from the worst effects of slumps. Political leaders also tried to tighten their control over central banks to assure that this newly acquired discretion would be exercised in the right way. In the United States, a succession of presidents—from Roosevelt to Nixon—sought to appoint Federal Reserve chairmen who seemed likely to take direction on the setting of interest rates. In the United Kingdom, meanwhile, political control over monetary policy was increased by a government takeover of the Bank of England in 1946.

Governments also promised that fiscal policy—the business of taxing and spending—would be tailored to counteract the boom-and-bust tendencies of a free-market economy. Even for Franklin Roosevelt, this was a substantial change. Roosevelt won the presidency in 1932 on a promise to balance the budget through "an immediate and drastic reduction of government expenditures."[93] At the time, Roosevelt was merely reflecting the conventional wisdom that parsimony was a virtue, even during depressions. By the end of the war, this conventional wisdom had changed. It was now accepted that governments had a duty to "prime the pump" during downturns by a "deliberate unbalancing" of their budgets.[94] Here, then, was a raft of changes that offered protection from the vagaries of a free-market economy. Government programs such as old-age pensions, health and unemployment insurance, and income support would protect individuals from many of the most serious life risks. Meanwhile governments would take on responsibility for active management of the economy as a whole, using fiscal and monetary policy to avoid slumps and booms. The roller coaster would come to an end. The main causes of economic unrest would finally be controlled.

A final reform offered an assurance that the whole package of policy adjustments would not be reversed. This was a clearing away of obstacles to union organizing. In the United States, union membership increased from 7 percent of the workforce in 1930 to 28 percent by the early 1950s, while in Britain it doubled from 22 to 44 percent. This meant that workers had more power to negotiate in the workplace. But it also gave them more power in voting booths as well. In 1965 the head of the AFL-CIO, the major trade union federation in the United States, boasted that "the stated goals of the administration and of Congress, on the one hand, and of the labor movement, on the other, are identical."[95] In Britain, even Conservative governments in these years were wary about antagonizing organized labor.

Herbert Spencer, the classical liberal who complained about interventions of the British parliament in the late nineteenth century, would have been aghast at the concessions made by Western governments in the wake of the Great Depression. Indeed, many of Spencer's intellectual heirs *were* aghast. The Austrian economist Friedrich von Hayek thought that the obsession with economic planning would lead to the complete extinguishment of human liberty. But this was a minority view. For most people, the changes that were undertaken in the wake of the Great Depression were the only sure way of preventing social and political upheaval. "For the sake of peace in the world, and in the interest of our internal security," said a speaker at a national farmers' conference in Oregon in 1946, "we cannot risk a depression in this country."[96]

3

The Market Comes Back

If we have learned anything from the long, bloody history of capitalism, it is this: economic policy is not something that is safely left to economists. An economic policy that performs very poorly does not have just an adverse effect on national accounts. In severe cases, it produces political and social disruption. Governments must have the institutions that enable them to manage this sort of disruption. Otherwise social order is threatened. This was the main lesson of the first liberal age. By the 1950s, American and British governments had adopted a bundle of reforms designed to maintain the social order. They took some actions that most people would say fall squarely in the field of economics, such as new restraints on finance and new tools for overall management of the economy. They also adopted some policies that we might say fall within the terrain of social policy or social justice. And they also applied some measures, such as better policing capabilities and stricter laws on demonstrations and protests, that do not seem at first glance to have much to do with economics at all. But all of these reforms constituted a coherent single package. They served the common purpose of protecting society from the risk of disorder that was associated with free-market capitalism.

In the last decades of the twentieth century—roughly from 1975 onward—this package began to unravel. Led by politicians like Ronald Reagan in the United States and Margaret Thatcher in Britain, governments in many countries began to disassemble controls on their economies. Tariffs and other barriers to trade were reduced and a great shift in the structure of global manufacturing began. In 1975, the total value of world trade was equal to roughly one third of world GDP. This increased to two-thirds of world GDP by 2008. The scale of trade flows in the newly liberalized global economy was staggering. At the high point of the first liberal age, shortly before the First World War, the busiest port in the world was London, which handled 40 million tons of cargo a year. In the neoliberal age, the busiest ports were in East Asia. Combined, the ports of Singapore, Shanghai, and Hong Kong handled more than 1 billion tons of cargo in 2009.

There was a similar transformation in the organization of financial services. In the United States and elsewhere, restrictions on financial institutions were loosened, and controls on cross-border lending and investment were removed. One result was a massive increase in value of global cross-border capital flows, from less than 1 percent of world GDP in 1980 to 12 percent of GDP in 2006. The value of foreign currency exchange on an average day in 2010 matched the total value of annual global production in the heyday of the first liberal age. Within the United States, the economic clout of the financial sector also increased. By the early 2000s, the share of GDP that was accounted for by financial and related services had reached levels not seen since before the Great Depression.

As trade and finance were liberalized, other tools for managing the economy were also being dismantled. Before 1980, it had been generally accepted that politicians ought to have control over fiscal and monetary policymaking, and that they should use those powers to smooth out peaks and troughs in the economy. In the field of fiscal policy—the business of taxing and spending—the orthodoxy had been that politicians should run deficits in hard times and surpluses in good times. "If private demand should flag and falter," *Time* magazine explained to its readers in 1965, "then it has to be revived by the only force strong enough to lift consumption: the government."[97] Similarly, the orthodoxy said that politicians should direct central banks to lower interest rates in bad times, and raise them during booms.

But neoliberals were skeptical about the capacity of politicians to wield their influence over fiscal policy intelligently. They argued that politicians, always trying to appease voters, failed to exercise discipline in good times, with the result that the debt built up in hard times was never paid off. And they argued that citizens had learned the game. When politicians ran deficits in hard times, people would start saving for possible future taxes, thus undermining the purpose of stimulus spending. Given these difficulties, neoliberals concluded that the best policy was a strict focus on budget balance in good times and bad times, with less concern about using taxing and spending to manage the overall economy.

Neoliberals were equally skeptical about the ability of politicians to make intelligent decisions about monetary policy. Neoliberals said that politicians could not resist the temptation to accelerate the economy by maintaining low interest rates even during good times, which resulted in nothing but corrosive inflation. The answer was to restrict political influence over monetary policy severely. The British government restored independence to its central bank, the Bank of England, in 1998. In the United States, the de facto autonomy of the Federal Reserve also increased steadily throughout the neoliberal age. By the early 2000s, the longtime chairman of the Federal Reserve, Alan Greenspan, was widely regarded as one of the most powerful people in Washington.

A final component of the neoliberal program was an assault on key aspects of the social safety net that had been constructed in the wake of the Great Depression. The political scientist Jacob Hacker has called this part of the neoliberal program "the great risk shift"—a political project aimed at transferring economic risk from government back onto the "fragile balance sheets of workers and their families."[98] In the United States, there were ongoing efforts to limit federal support for the poor and unemployed. Neoliberals also launched proposals to eliminate government-run unemployment insurance entirely, replacing it with a system of personally managed unemployment protection accounts. Similarly, Social Security would have been replaced with a system of personally run retirement accounts, while Medicare would have been replaced with a mixed system of privately purchased health insurance and government coverage for truly catastrophic health problems.

Direct assaults on the social safety net had limited success, both in the United Kingdom and the United States. As a share of GDP, social spending by government in both countries in 2000 was comparable to what it had been in 1980. In fact, neoliberals should be glad that this part of their reform project failed. If the social safety net had been cut back as much as they wanted, public anger after the crash of 2008 would have been much more intense. Battered though it was, the social safety net continued to perform the role for which it had been designed. It helped to protect people from extreme hardship, and consequently discouraged unrest during hard times.

Still, there is no doubt that neoliberals enjoyed greater success in other domains. After 1975, the global economy was fundamentally transformed. By the end of the millennium, paeans about the triumph of free-market capitalism were commonplace. In 2002 the political scientist Michael Mandelbaum argued that free-market ideology had "conquered the world."[99] This was the moment at which Schumpeter's idea of creative destruction—in its benign and bloodless form—enjoyed its unexpected revival. But few proponents of the neoliberal model seemed to worry, as Schumpeter himself might have worried, that the revival of laissez faire principles would also heighten the risk of periodic social disruption.

Two Myths about Peaceful Reform

In fact, many economists who advocated for free-market reforms denied that they were likely to create a significant risk of social unrest. Consequently they did not seriously consider how that unrest would be managed. Consider, for example, the substance of the Washington Consensus. This was a term coined in 1990 by John Williamson, an economist at a prominent Washington think tank. It was meant to describe the short list of reforms that "technocratic Washington" (how Williams described the community of experts in the International Monetary Fund, World Bank, and key U.S. agencies) usually imposed on developing countries as a condition of receiving aid. In short, the Washington Consensus told developing countries that they should expand the realm of "free-market capitalism" by dismantling government controls over the economy.[100] As Schumpeter might have said, its aim was to unleash the power of creative destruction. But the Washington Consensus said nothing about preserving public order after market forces had been unleashed. The instruction manual for liberalization that was given to other countries included no directions on improving police and paramilitary forces, for example. It did not occur to technocratic Washington that directions like this would be necessary.

Technocratic Washington was captured by two myths, both of which encouraged the belief that Schumpeter was wrong, and market reforms could be undertaken without a significant risk of disorder. We can call the first of these delusions the myth of the rising tide. It takes its name from a slogan that was popular in Washington throughout the heyday of neoliberal reform: "A rising tide lifts all boats." This was meant to convey the idea that market reforms would generate so much new wealth that no one would be worse off than they had been before. Granted, some people might get richer faster than others, but even the poorest would see benefits from reform. Moreover the gains from growth would be so substantial that it would be easy to compensate people who suffered losses as government controls over the economy were removed. And because no large class of people would be substantially worse off than they were before, the risks of unrest would be negligible.

The myth of the rising tide addressed the everyday workings of a market economy. It said that there was nothing to worry about as creative destruction was unleashed to do its work. But there was another way in which the risk of unrest could be increased. In the first liberal age, the economy had behaved like a roller coaster, often plunging into slumps that were marked by spasms of serious disorder. In that age, many people regarded this overall instability as an unavoidable feature of a lightly regulated capitalist system. Was there not a risk that the cycle of boom and slump might return in the neoliberal age, reviving the risk of periodic spasms of severe unrest?

Washington's technocrats had an answer to this question. We can call it the myth of the stable market. It involved a complete rejection of the notion that liberalization meant a return to the boom-and-slump cycle. The new school of free-market economics emphasized the rationality of the free market, its efficiency in processing information, and its creativity in inventing new ways of diffusing risk. At the same time, new information technologies seemed to promise the instantaneous spread of information about market conditions around the globe. Operating with these presumptions, it was difficult for free-market advocates to see how a cycle of boom and slump could arise. Businessmen did not make reckless or ill-informed investments. They did not get caught up in herd behavior. They anticipated and planned for contingencies. Far from being regarded as intrinsically unstable, the modern free market was celebrated for its "self-stabilizing properties." As one academic argued in the journal *Foreign Affairs* in 1997:

> Modern economies operate differently than nineteenth-century and early twentieth-century industrial economies. Changes in technology, ideology, employment, and finance, along with the globalization of production and consumption, have reduced the volatility of economic activity in the industrialized world. For both empirical and theoretical reasons, in advanced industrial economies the waves of the business cycle may be becoming more like ripples.[101]

The myth of the stable market had many other high-profile adherents. Federal Reserve chairman Alan Greenspan boasted in 2002 about the "reduction in the volatility of output and in the frequency and amplitude of business cycles. . . . Shocks are more readily absorbed than in decades past."[102] And a 2004 report by the investment bank Goldman Sachs concurred, arguing that market reforms had "reduce[d] the volatility of the economy. Recessions are less frequent and milder when they occur. As a result, upward spikes in the unemployment rate have occurred less frequently and have become less severe."[103]

These two myths performed the same function. In essence, they said that Schumpeter and Polanyi were wrong, and that the history of the first liberal age was irrelevant: the restoration of free-market policies did not imply an increase in the risk of unrest as well. But as the neoliberal age progressed, neither of these myths held up well. Developing countries that imported the neoliberal model frequently found that implementation of free-market policies led to problems of disorder. At first, the tendency of technocrats in leading free-market nations like the United States was to discount evidence that challenged the two myths. But the steady accretion of experience made this increasingly difficult to do, especially when the financial crisis of 2008 brought problems of unrest to the developed world as well.

The myth of the rising tide, for example, grossly underestimated the pain that could be inflicted as developing countries removed controls on their economies. Perhaps, in the long run, the rising tide lifted all boats. In the short run, some boats were unambiguously sunk. People lost their jobs as state-owned enterprises were closed down and private firms collapsed under pressure of foreign competition. Real incomes deteriorated as controls on the price of food and fuel were removed. And even if the poor were better off after reform, they were stung by the more rapid advance of the middle and upper classes. The positive feeling that came from making progress over time was washed out by resentment over the fact that others were doing much better. "Inequality probably matters quite a lot to human happiness," the British economist Adair Turner belatedly acknowledged in 2012, "and the problems created by inequality cannot be swept away by growth."[104]

Not only was the myth of the rising tide contestable in theory; increasingly, it was belied by experience. In Latin America, for example, the transition to free-market policies was marked by pervasive unrest. The governments of Argentina and Bolivia each declared a state of siege to restore order after the adoption of neoliberal policies in the late 1980s. Similarly, Venezuela imposed martial law to quell massive protests against neoliberal reforms in 1989. ("The armed forces were entrusted with controlling the situation," the Inter-American Court of Human Rights later explained. "Members of the armed forces opened fire against crowds and against homes.... There was a common pattern of behavior characterized by the disproportionate use of the armed forces in the poorer residential districts.")[105] The Dominican Republic deployed the army to stop protests over similar reforms in 1995. Paraguay declared a state of emergency to contain protests over neoliberal policies in 2002, and Guatemalan protesters were "brutally dispersed" by national police following protests against liberalization in 2005.[106]

But the most powerful repudiation of the myth of the rising tide might have been provided by China. It began its own experiments with free-market principles after Deng Xiaoping's ascension to the post of paramount leader in 1978. The Chinese government reduced support for state-owned enterprises, encouraged the growth of private industries, and removed restrictions on international trade and investment. Of course, the conversion to the market principles was not complete. The Chinese state was careful to retain control over many instruments for guiding the national economy. Still, the transformation of the Chinese economy was "a true miracle."[107] Between 1980 and 2010, it grew by 9 percent a year, driven heavily by exports from its booming southern provinces. China never experienced a massive slump in those three decades.

In the very worst years of that period (1989–90), the economy still grew by 4 percent annually.

In China, the tide was rising very quickly. Still, this was not a peaceful transformation. For many years, China's Ministry of Public Security estimated the number of "mass incidents" that occurred across the country annually. These ranged from small marches to larger strikes, demonstrations, and riots. The Central Party School said that they were "the manifestation of the people's increasingly confrontational and sharpened internal conflicts."[108] There were roughly ten thousand mass incidents a year in the early 1990s. By 2005, this number had grown to ninety thousand—or one mass incident every six minutes. Only a small proportion of these incidents were triggered by discontent over authoritarian rule or ethnic conflicts. Most arose out of the process of market-based modernization. Unrest increased as laborers were dismissed from declining state industries in northeastern China; as migrants who had crowded into the new industrial heartland of the Pearl River Delta became frustrated over oppressive working conditions; as peasants grew angry over the expropriation of land for industrial development and the pollution that spilled from new factories; and as wageworkers in major cities were pushed aside by the growing number of wealthy and privileged Chinese.

Some of these incidents became dangerously large. In 2002, for example, tens of thousands of workers protested against layoffs from state-owned firms in the northeastern city of Liaoyang. It was the biggest demonstration in China since Tiananmen Square, and authorities responded with a massive deployment of riot police. There was an even larger protest in southwestern China in 2004, as 100,000 peasants fought with police over the expropriation of land for a hydroelectric project. Ten thousand paramilitary police were sent to aid beleaguered local forces. Thousands of paramilitary police were also required to restore peace in Dong-yang in 2005, after protests about pollution from nearby chemical plants. In 2011, police laid siege to the village of Wukan, which had been taken over by villagers angry over land expropriation. Neither Schumpeter nor Polanyi would have been surprised by recent Chinese history. British and American experience in the nineteenth century had already shown them the falsity of the myth of the rising tide. Rapid growth was not a guarantor of domestic peace—on the contrary, it could be the trigger for widespread unrest. In China, Communist Party theorists reached the same conclusion but expressed it in different terms. Borrowing the language of Mao Zedong, they worried about the "internal contradictions" generated by free-market policies. China had entered a "golden age of development," editors at the state-run Xinhua News Agency wrote in 2004—but also risked collapsing into a "contradictions-stricken age" of chaos.[109]

The myth of the stable market was equally flawed. It was supposed to provide reassurance that there could never be major economic collapses, and thus not major spasms of unrest, as there had been so frequently before the Second World War. Evidence against this myth also mounted throughout the neoliberal age, although it took some time for free-market advocates to acknowledge it. It was not until the financial crisis of 2008 that the myth of the stable market finally collapsed.

One early sign that the myth might be misguided was provided by the experience of Mexico in the early 1990s. In the late 1980s and early 1990s, the Mexican economy was supercharged by a massive inflow of money sent by foreign investors excited by the government's liberalization program. Then a series of events stoked doubts among investors about the direction of the nation's politics. The inflow of capital stopped suddenly, and Mexican borrowers could not make payments on their foreign loans. In an attempt to reassure overseas creditors, the Mexican government introduced a tough austerity program. The International Monetary Fund praised Mexico for responding "promptly and effectively to economic and financial developments."[110] But clashes between protesters and riot police became frequent events in Mexico City. Two hundred thousand people flouted a ban on the capital's traditional May Day march in 1995. Protesters assailed the presidential residence, shut down the stock exchange, blocked highways, and occupied universities.

Mexico's crisis could have been taken as a warning that international finance was not as steady and farsighted as technocratic Washington imagined it to be. That is, it could have been construed as evidence about the fragility of the theory underlying liberalization itself. But this is not how the Mexican crisis was interpreted at the time. Instead, it was viewed as an anomaly that happened because of the immaturity of Mexican institutions. Critics said that Mexican banks had been careless in extending credit, Mexican regulators had been ineffectual in overseeing the banks, and Mexican politicians had mismanaged the task of maintaining popular support. In short, this was a problem in Mexico, not in the model.

Later calamities were discounted in similar ways. A program of liberalization in Thailand was followed by real estate and stock market bubbles that collapsed in 1997, leading to a series of national economic crises throughout East Asia. These were accompanied by intense unrest. In Bangkok and Seoul, riot police fought bloody battles against unemployed workers, while Jakarta was overwhelmed by rioting that led to the collapse of the Indonesian government. The East Asian financial crisis, like the Mexican crisis, might have been taken as a warning about the skittishness of investor behavior and instability of the system of liberalized finance.

Instead, it was treated as another anomaly, caused by the flawed execution of free-market policies in the region. The crisis, Paul Krugman explained in 1998, had revealed "the dark underside to 'Asian values.'"[111]

Three years later, Argentina provided more evidence against the myth of the stable market. Like Mexico, Argentina launched a liberalization program in the 1990s and was rewarded by capital inflows that stoked an economic boom and a rapid increase in government indebtedness. After the East Asian crisis, however, investors fled Argentina. The boom ended, and the country tottered toward default. The Argentine government struggled to reassure foreign lenders by introducing austerity policies, but this triggered massive unrest. In 2001, 13 million workers joined in a nationwide general strike against the measures. The credit rating agency Moody's downgraded Argentine debt, citing "intense opposition from diverse social and political groups . . . [to] strict fiscal austerity."[112] The flight of foreign investors from Argentina intensified. So did unrest. "We are dissolving into instability," an Argentine economist complained in December 2001. "We are on the verge of a total social eruption."[113] The next day, President Fernando De La Rúa declared a state of siege. Outside the presidential mansion, police on horseback charged the crowds. But the protests could not be contained, and De La Rúa soon resigned, escaping by helicopter from the presidential palace. Argentina defaulted a few days later. Again, the Argentine crisis could have been regarded as a warning sign about dangers inherent in the liberalized global economy. It was not. Instead, free-market reformers blamed Argentina's politicians and its "weak political institutions" for the debacle.[114]

"Financial crises," Federal Reserve chairman Ben Bernanke said much later, "were things that happened in emerging markets and not in developed countries."[115] In Washington, the myth of the stable market persisted. It did not collapse until the financial crisis of 2008 hit the United States and many other advanced economies. Finally, the crises that had afflicted other nations before 2008 were recognized as part of a pattern—a "well-worn script"[116]—that was now playing out in rich democracies as well. "Recent experience," the *Financial Times* columnist Martin Wolf concluded in 2012, "has underlined the thesis that there are deep, inherent instabilities in a market economy with an open, unregulated financial system."[117]

The myth of the stable market mattered because it provided a guarantee that free-market nations would never be exposed to periods of debilitating unrest. When the myth collapsed, so did the guarantee. After 2008, many countries in the developed world were wracked with disorder. One of the first to suffer was Latvia, whose government had attempted to reassure foreign lenders by introducing a stringent austerity program. In January 2009, a protest by ten thousand people at the Latvian parliament building turned into a full-scale riot. The Latvian government fell five weeks later. There was also trouble in neighboring Lithuania. Protesters "launched two attempts to force their way into the Seimas [the Lithuanian Parliament building]," the *Baltic News Service* reported. "Public Security Service units ... used rubber bullets, tear gas and trained dogs to disperse [the] demonstration."[118] The International Monetary Fund lauded Lithuania's prime minister for "courage and skill" in reviving investor confidence.[119] A few days after the Lithuanian demonstrations, protesters also stormed the Icelandic parliament. They blamed the conservative government of Prime Minister Geir Haarde for coddling bankers. For the first time in sixty years, Iceland's police used tear gas to control the crowd. Haarde's government announced it would hold early elections.

At the end of January 2009, the contagion of unrest jumped to a major economy. More than 1 million workers participated in a general strike in France. One union leader called it "a cry of anger" against rising unemployment.[120] There was an even larger general strike in March 2009. The following year, union leaders organized a succession of protests against the Sarkozy government's proposal to restrict public pensions. Riot police used rubber bullets and tear gas to quell violence in many cities in October 2010. President Sarkozy was defeated in elections in early 2012.

Southern European economies were more seriously afflicted. Unable to sell its bonds and dependent on emergency aid from the International Monetary Fund and European Union, the Greek government adopted a severe austerity budget in 2010. Thousands rallied in Athens in May 2010, surrounding the parliament and setting fire to the finance ministry. Three died after a private bank was firebombed. "Our country came to the brink of the abyss," President Karolos Papoulias said at the time. "The big challenge we face is to maintain social cohesion and peace."[121] Three months later, Spanish unions called a general strike against austerity policies that the Socialist government had introduced to reassure jittery foreign investors. In November 2010, forty thousand university students marched in Ireland against cutbacks, occupying the finance ministry until they were ejected by riot police.

The cabinet minister responsible for Britain's police, Theresa May, was proud that her country escaped the wave of unrest. "The British public," she said in September 2010, "doesn't resort to violent unrest in the face of challenging economic circumstances."[122] Clearly, May did not read much history. Nor did she understand the public mood. Eight weeks later, thousands of university students protested against austerity measures. Some smashed the windows of the British Treasury. Four months after that, a quarter million people marched in London to protest budget cuts. And in August 2011, thousands of people in depressed suburbs of London and other major cities engaged in five days of rioting that resulted in four deaths. British police admitted that they were caught off guard. "We have been going through a period where we have not seen that sort of violent disorder," the head of London's police force said. "We are into a different period I am afraid. We will be putting far more assets in place to ensure we can respond properly."[123] This policy of intensive policing had the intended effect. British protests were more muted than they had been during earlier crises. "I hear a lot of people asking why there isn't more resistance going on," one activist complained in 2013. "Here's why. There was resistance, and it was brutally and systematically put down."[124]

But other countries did not manage unrest so efficiently. In Portugal, 300,000 people joined in a day of protest over cutbacks in March 2011. Moody's immediately lowered its rating of Portuguese government debt. In May 2011, tens of thousands gathered for more protests in Spain's major cities. Moody's announced that it would review its rating of Spanish debt because of "domestic factors" that were undermining the government's efforts to reduce spending. Later that year, there was more violence in Greece as police tried to clear a protesters' camp in central Athens. Moody's warned investors that Greece was suffering from "austerity fatigue."

By then, the world was entering the fourth year of the global economic crisis, and two facts were clear. The first was that neoliberals had vastly underestimated the potential for unrest that laid within the free-market model. At first, two myths—of the rising tide, and the stable market—had offered the assurance that the neoliberal age would be more peaceful than the first liberal age. But a quarter-century of experience eventually reaffirmed what Schumpeter, Polanyi, and many others had observed seven decades ago. Laissez faire policies promoted growth—but at the same time, they increased the likelihood of disorder, either through the routine operation of creative destruction, and because the instability of the system as a whole.

But there was a second fact that was also clear: there were exceptions to this pattern of unrest. Two prominent exceptions were the vanguard states of market reform. The United States, and to a lesser degree the United Kingdom, escaped the serious unrest that afflicted so many other advanced nations after 2008. Clearly something had been done in those two countries that had the effect of containing disorder. There was a method of keeping the peace that was not articulated explicitly in the checklist of market-oriented reforms that had been given to other countries in the heyday of the neoliberal era. But what exactly was this unstated formula for reconciling free-market policies with the demand for social order?

4

The New Method of Controlling Disorder

Together, the United States and the United Kingdom formed the vanguard of the neoliberal revolution. Politicians in both countries took free-market principles seriously. But they were not entirely bound by doctrine. Throughout this period, leading politicians in both countries also experimented with methods of avoiding and controlling unrest. This was an intensely pragmatic exercise, involving experimentation over many years—much as the response to unrest during the first liberal age was, as Karl Polanyi observed in 1944, a "purely practical and pragmatic" project that spanned decades.[125] In some ways, the task of avoiding unrest required diversions from core neoliberal principles, as well as generally accepted notions about how a democracy is supposed to operate. As a result it was neither easy nor politically prudent to summarize succinctly what was contained within the formula for maintaining social order. But there certainly was a formula, whose effectiveness was demonstrated in these two countries throughout the neoliberal age, and particularly after the financial crisis of 2008.

Breaking the Unions

In the earliest phase of the economic crisis, the spirits of many American progressives were buoyed by a labor action in Chicago that seemed to portend a larger wave of labor militancy against the free-market excesses of the preceding three decades. Republic Windows and Doors was a small manufacturer that declared bankruptcy in December 2008 after Bank of America canceled its line of credit. Two hundred workers occupied the plant, demanding severance pay and health benefits. Bank of America had already received billions of dollars in emergency aid from the federal government and was at that moment one of the most loathed institutions in the country. It quickly joined with other creditors to create a $1.8 million fund to aid Republic's workers, while another company took over the firm's operations. "It was a huge victory," said Kari Lyderson, a writer for the *Washington Post*.[126] Union organizers saw the Republic protest as the "harbinger of a revitalized and reinvigorated labor movement in the U.S."[127]

But the Republic protest was not a harbinger of labor activism. In fact, the experience of the next several years showed how much the labor movement had been debilitated as a result of three decades of neoliberal policies. In the United States, the proportion of the American workforce that belongs to a trade union dropped from 22 percent in 1980 to 11 percent in 2011. However this aggregate statistic masked two distinct trends. Within the public sector, unionization rates had increased sharply in the late 1970s, and remained stable (at about 37 percent of the workforce) for the whole of the following three decades. Within the private sector, meanwhile, membership plummeted to only 7 percent of the workforce by 2011. The pattern was similar in the United Kingdom. There, the overall rate of unionization dropped from 50 percent of the workforce in 1980 to 26 percent in 2011. Again, however, trends differed in the private and public sectors. In 2011, 57 percent of Britain's public sector workforce was represented by unions. But the unionization rate in the private sector had plummeted to only 14 percent.

The atrophy of private sector unionism in the United States and Britain was a direct result of shifts in government attitudes toward organized labor in both countries, as well as the indirect result of neoliberal economic policies. In the early 1980s, the Reagan administration and Thatcher government both engaged in high-profile conflicts that signaled their determination to reduce the power of organized labor. In the United States, the critical struggle was between the newly elected Reagan administration and striking air traffic controllers in the summer of 1981, while in Britain, the defining moment was the Thatcher government's conflict with striking workers in the coal industry in 1984–85. In both cases, conservative leaders broke the union, and then consolidated their victories with changes in law that undercut the labor movement's ability to organize workers. Trade liberalization weakened unions even further by making it easier for businesses to move to locations with weaker labor laws.

The result was that organized labor no longer had the capacity to mobilize dissent that it enjoyed thirty years ago. One sign of this was a dramatic reduction in the number of major strikes. On average between 1947 and 1980, the United States experienced 300 major strikes (each involving at least one thousand workers) every year. Between 1980 and 2000, that number declined to 50 a year, and in the first decade of the new millennium, it declined again to 17 a year. The weakness of organized labor was illustrated vividly during the economic crisis itself. There were only 54 major work stoppages in the United States between 2009 and 2012. By contrast there were 428 major stoppages during the milder three-year recession of 1981–82, and 611 during the even milder recession of 1957–58. "The strike," one student of the labor movement wrote in 2012, "has virtually disappeared from American life."[128] The same could be said of the United Kingdom. There was an average of 227 work stoppages in progress in Britain in any month between 1947 and 1980. But that number dropped to 68 in 1980–2000, and then to only 15 a month in 2001–11. The decline of union power involves more than a reduction in strike activity. It has also led to an erosion of labor influence within the political process. In Britain, the waning influence of labor was evidenced by a change in Labour Party rules in 1993 that limited the power of unions in selecting party leaders. In the United States, meanwhile, organized labor attempted to counter the impact of declining membership by developing better techniques of lobbying and political campaigning. By 2010, however, it was clear that this strategy had reached the limits of its usefulness. Friends of the labor movement doubted whether it would be possible to remain a significant influence in American legislatures if the long-term erosion of union membership was not checked.[129]

The capacity of unions to exercise political pressure by organizing mass protests collapsed as well. To appreciate this change, it is useful to turn the clock back to the summer of 1981, when the Reagan administration began its now-famous struggle with striking air traffic controllers. American union leaders immediately recognized that the administration's decision to fire the striking workers was the opening skirmish in a much larger assault on labor power. One union head predicted "terrible misery for the whole labor movement, public and private, unless we recognize the gravity of the challenge and muster the solidarity to reverse it."[130] Within weeks, the major unions organized two major protests against the Reagan administration's policies. The first—a Labor Day march in New York City—drew 100,000 people. The second, held in Washington two weeks later, was even larger. One quarter of a million people came to the capital to join the protest, which was called Solidarity Day, in a nod to the workers' movement that was challenging Poland's communist regime. It was the largest demonstration in Washington since the civil rights and antiwar demonstrations of the 1960s and 1970s. But the Solidarity Day crowds were more blue collar than those of a decade earlier. "The soundtrack was Country and Western, not folk rock," the *New York Times* reported, "and the marchers tended to smoke Marlboros, not marijuana."[131]

Solidarity Day "proved one thing about the unions," another journalist said at the time, "they still know how to organize."[132] Some leaders hoped that the Washington demonstration would be the prelude to an even larger campaign against the Reagan administration's free-market policies. These hopes were quickly dashed. As union membership declined, so did the capacity of labor leaders to organize protests that were as large and diverse as the Solidarity Day demonstration had been. This was illustrated almost thirty years later, in the wake of the financial crisis of 2007–8, when union leaders joined with other progressive groups to hold a similar demonstration in Washington. The 2010 rally drew only a fraction of the crowd that unions had gathered three decades earlier: in fact, the *Washington Post* estimated that there were more people gathered in Nashville's Vanderbilt Stadium to watch the LSU Tigers crush the Vanderbilt Commodores that weekend. The 2010 rally did not fall short because people were suffering less. On the contrary, conditions were worse in October 2010 than they had been in September 1981. It fell short because the union movement no longer had such an extensive infrastructure for mobilizing protest over economic grievances.

Admittedly, public sector unions did play an important role in organizing protests against cutbacks in spending by state governments after 2008. Almost all state governments have constitutional or statutory obligations to balance their budgets, and most made deep cuts in spending as tax revenues dropped in the first two years

of the economic crisis. Many states laid off workers, reduced sala-
ries and benefits, and considered new laws to weaken the bargain-
ing power of unions representing state employees[133]—particularly
after the Republican Party won control of a larger share of state
legislatures in the 2010 elections. In Wisconsin, thousands of people protested at the state capitol against legislation that weakened
union rights. Jesse Jackson told protesters in Madison that this
would be "a Martin Luther King moment, a Gandhi moment . . .
the first round of a longer battle to renew the integrity of our nation."[134] But the Wisconsin protest might have been the high point
of labor resistance to state austerity measures during the crisis, and
it did not succeed in stopping Wisconsin's antilabor law.

More broadly, labor activism during the economic crisis actually had an unexpected effect. According to the Gallup Poll, public
approval of labor unions in the United States dropped markedly
during the economic crisis, to the lowest levels recorded since
data was first collected in 1936. Even among people identifying
themselves as Democrats or independents, support for unions
declined.[135] The proportion of respondents who told Gallup that
they would like unions to have *less* influence rose from 28 percent
in 2007 to 42 percent by 2011.[136] This shift in attitudes after 2008
was a result of the fact that labor unionism had become a pre-
dominantly public sector phenomenon. Unions were now viewed
as obstacles to the reduction of state government spending, which
most people saw as the preferred alternative to higher taxes, and
union activism was more likely to be regarded as an impediment
to overall economic recovery. Public sector unions could not rely
on the goodwill of voters who were themselves members of the
broader labor movement—for the simple reason that the vast
majority of American households no longer included any union
members at all.

The Limits of Networked Protest

By the end of the 1990s, many progressives were hoping that technological change would enable new methods of mobilization that would compensate for the waning power of big unions. The internet dramatically reduced the barriers to collaboration among activists and allowed the formation of expansive protest networks. These networks lacked the command-and-control structure of the old-line labor movement. At first, this did not seem to be an impediment to their effectiveness. The new technologies promised a new mode of leaderless coordination. As David Graeber, an anthropologist who was a prominent advocate of the new form of protest, explained:

> [T]he interconnections of communication are such that you can imagine people not just communicating but acting, and acting damn effectively, without leadership, a secretariat, without even formal information channels. It's a little like ants meeting in an ant-heap, all waving their antennae at each other, and information just gets around—even though there's no chain of command or even hierarchical information structure. Of course it would be impossible without the Internet.[137]

The protests in Seattle against the World Trade Organization in 1999 were the moment at which the old style of hierarchically organized protest was displaced by the new style of protest by decentralized networks. AFL-CIO president John Sweeney had promised to rally tens of thousands of workers in Seattle for a "confrontation" over trade liberalization.[138] But the labor turnout was lower than expected, and at the last minute union leaders decided to avoid a direct confrontation with police guarding the WTO's conference facilities. It was another group of protesters, a loose network of progressive and radical groups, moving quickly and using unorthodox tactics to block the streets, that caught the Seattle police off guard, shut down the meeting, and seized the headlines. The protesters who formed this network were the "true heroes" of Seattle, said Alexander Cockburn and Jeffrey St. Clair.[139]

The activist Naomi Klein argued that Seattle was "a coming-out party" for a decentralized, nonhierarchical movement dedicated to opposing neoliberal policies.[140] The new model of antiglobalization activism, Klein said in 2000, mirrored "the organic, decentralized pathways of the internet—[it is] the internet come to life."[141] In the next decade, this loosely structured movement besieged a series of major international conferences. Tens of thousands of protesters gathered at annual meetings of the International Monetary Fund and World Bank, summits for leaders of the major economies, and sessions to negotiate new liberalization treaties. It was estimated that 30,000 people were mobilized to protest at a free trade summit held in Quebec City in April 2001, and more than 100,000 at a meeting of G8 leaders in Genoa three months later. An underlying irony was that this rising antiglobalization movement relied so heavily on information technologies that had emerged, in large part, because of their usefulness in organized globalized systems of production and finance. It appeared as though the liberalized global economy had inadvertently created the conditions necessary for the emergence of a powerful new countermovement. The demise of organized labor might be lamented, but it seemed as though the task of resisting liberalization could be carried on by these new "decentralized peer networks of the digital age."[142]

The Occupy movement that arose in September 2011 was built on the same model of leaderless, technology-enabled mobilization. None of the Occupy encampments that were set up in major cities had a hierarchical governance structure. Each was guided by a general assembly that made decisions on the basis of consensus.

Graeber said that the movement was built on "anarchist principles of mutual aid and self-recognition."[143] And in its early phases, the Occupy movement appeared to be a spectacular success. Opinion polls in the autumn of 2011 showed broad public concern about inequality and other problems that had been emphasized by the Occupiers. "One thing is starkly evident," said one sympathetic study in February 2012, "the protest has given birth to America's most important progressive movement since the civil rights marches half a century ago."[144] Many other people made equally extravagant claims about the influence of the Occupy protests in early 2012.

Within a year, though, the movement had begun to fade into history. In retrospect, the movement suffered from fatal weaknesses, some of which were intrinsic to the model of decentralized, consensus-based mobilization. One was the inability to formulate a coherent statement of what the protesters' goals should be. Certainly, there was a broadly shared and roughly articulated indignation over the inequities generated by the neoliberal project. But the Occupy encampments could not produce a more concrete view of what an alternative set of policies would look like. There were some Occupiers who refused to articulate demands for reform at all, arguing that this would concede "the legitimacy of existing political institutions."[145] The larger problem was that it was impossible to agree on reforms without abandoning the decentralized and consensus-based model of organization on which Occupy Wall Street, and the antiglobalization movement more broadly, depended. There was always a minority ready to block any conceivable reform proposal.

For similar reasons, the movement could not devise a strategy for building broader support for its goals. The Occupy protesters were a small group, and in many respects unrepresentative of the broader population. (Studies at the major encampments suggested that Occupiers were younger, less racially diverse, better educated, and more politically radical than Americans in general.) To actually achieve a change in the world, it would have been necessary to build alliances with other politically influential constituencies. But many Occupy protesters were deeply resistant to the work of negotiation and compromise that alliance-building would have entailed. This would have required delegating authority to leaders, which a critical number of Occupiers were unprepared to countenance. At the same time, an influential minority of Occupiers blocked attempts to distance their movement from more militant elements, whose tactics—such as vandalism and open confrontation with police—alienated the wider public. These difficulties were not unique to Occupy. The Occupy protests merely provided a further illustration of difficulties that had plagued the antiglobalization movement in its short history since Seattle. The model of leaderless resistance had its limitations.

These limitations went beyond the inability to articulate and pursue a coherent agenda. Another problem was the inability, at critical moments, to mobilize protest in a timely way. Since the mid-1990s, advocates of neoliberalism had unwittingly performed an important function for antiglobalizers by providing a convenient focus for their protests. The decentralized protest network always knew when and where to gather: at the next G8 or G20 summit, the next trade conference, or the next meeting of the International Monetary Fund. When politicians did not set the time and place for protest, however, the antiglobalization movement was at a loss. This is one reason why the Occupy protests were so long in coming. (Many people wondered about this. "Simply to point to these welcome demonstrations," wrote the political scientist Robert McChesney, "begs the question of why it has taken so long for such protest to emerge.")[146] When Occupy Wall Street set up its camp in Manhattan in September 2011, the economic crisis was in its third year. Economic distress was much more intense that it had been in September 1981, when the AFL-CIO organized Solidarity Day. And yet the resistance movement had not been mobilized, because it lacked a leadership structure that could make an authoritative call for action. It was a Canadian anticonsumerism magazine, *Adbusters*, that finally did the job, by issuing a call for protesters to set up tents in Manhattan on September 17, 2011.

For all of these reasons, the new forms of social mobilization were imperfect substitutes for old forms, such as the labor movement. And there was one other critical consideration. Governments quickly adapted their methods of policing to counter the new modes of protests. In its after-action report on the 1999 WTO conference, the Seattle police force conceded that it had been caught off guard by the "new paradigm of disruptive protest." But the report also predicted that the WTO protests would "come to be recognized as a watershed event . . . of considerable interest to law enforcement agencies throughout the nation and the world."[147] This prediction was quickly fulfilled. In 2006 a leading U.S. police research organization described the Seattle protests as a "defining moment in how local law enforcement manages mass demonstrations."[148] Police forces overseas learned from Seattle as well. The techniques of control which they subsequently invented would severely curtail the disruptive potential of the new forms of protest that seized public attention in November 1999.

Strengthening the Police

In fact, politicians in the United States and United Kingdom had a special interest in policing throughout the neoliberal age.

This should not be a surprise: they had a similar interest during the first liberal age as well. But this is also evidence of the triumph of pragmatism over principle. After all, a critical aim of the neoliberal program was reducing the bloated public sector. "Spending is out of control," complained David Osborne, a prominent advocate of leaner government, in 1993. "The public is frustrated, angry, disgusted, and ready for change. . . . We are in for a decade of excruciating pain at state and local levels."[149] However, American police forces did not feel this pain. The Department of Justice estimates that public expenditure on policing by all levels of American government more than tripled, even after adjustment for inflation, between 1982 and 2009. A 2002 Justice Department study found that the number of police officers employed in major American cities increased by 17 percent between 1990 and 2000. In New York City alone, the uniformed force increased from thirty-one thousand to forty thousand officers in that decade.[150] New York Michael Bloomberg later boasted that he had "my own private army in the NYPD, which is the seventh-biggest army in the world."[151]

New York City's preoccupation with policing was partly a byproduct of free-market policies. As barriers to trade collapsed, manufacturers fled the city for lower-cost jurisdictions. The city lost three-quarters of a million jobs in manufacturing between 1966 and 2009. (Many other cities had the same experience.) As the sociologist Alex Vitale has noted, the loss of so many factory jobs lead to problems of poverty and urban decay that the city government, confronting a decline in tax revenues, could not address.[152] The result was an increase in homelessness and petty crime.

The city's economic recovery depended on the expansion of tourism, finance, and other services. This meant closer attention to the city's "urban brand"—the image that it projected to the world that made it attractive to tourists and professionals. "If a city is perceived as violent and unsafe," one specialist on urban branding explained, "obviously the city must combat crime and violence. . . . Solving the problem of crime improves a city's image."[153] So New York City's police force expanded even as other municipal services were cut back. At the same time, the police force adopted a strict policy of making arrests for minor offenses that contributed to the perception of disorder. This was "a new philosophy of urban social control," wrote Vitale, "that emphasized the centrality of maintaining order through aggressive zero-tolerance policing."[154]

The neoliberal era also saw a sharp rise in contributions from the U.S. federal government toward the cost of police services. This happened despite the larger drive for reduction of federal spending. In 1996, President Bill Clinton famously announced that "the era of big government is over." But Clinton also signed laws to pay for the addition of 150,000 police to American streets. In 2000 the Clinton White House claimed that it had increased funding for state and local law enforcement by 300 percent since 1993. Later, the federal government also began to routinely provide additional funding to cities hosting "national special security events"—such as the summit on free trade in the Americas held in Miami in 2003 and the economic summits that were scheduled for Washington in 2008, Pittsburgh in 2009, and Chicago in 2012. The money was used to defray the cost of bolstering police numbers, and also to improve capabilities that remained long after the event itself. The cities of Tampa and Charlotte received $100 million from the federal government to support policing for the 2012 Republican and Democratic conventions, both designated as special security events. Much of that money was spent on facilities and equipment, including communications and surveillance gear, a new command center for the Charlotte police force, and for the Tampa Police Department, an armored vehicle custom-built for urban operations.

Spending on police services in Britain increased throughout the neoliberal age as well. The Thatcher government was ruthless in reorganizing many parts of the British public sector, but not the police, whose services were recognized to be essential to contain labor unrest and inner-city rioting. The police, says P.A.J. Waddington, "were in the front line of a social revolution."[155] After the unrest of the early 1980s, the Thatcher government made a public commitment to increase police numbers and pay. Between 1988 and 1998, expenditure on British policing increased by 33 percent, even after adjustment for inflation.[156] The advent of a Labour government in 1997 did not reverse this trend. On the contrary, the government of Prime Minister Tony Blair tried to prove its toughness on law and order by launching another "decade of record investment in policing." The growth in expenditure happened, a recent study concludes, "because there was a political consensus . . . instead of any systemic profiling of need or impact analysis." By 2011 it could be safely concluded that British police have "never been better resourced . . . [with] more officers than ever before."[157]

Not only were there more police officers in Britain and the United States: they were better equipped for crowd control than ever before. Protesters who confronted police in the United States around 1970 usually saw officers who were dressed for normal duty, except with the addition of a light helmet. By the early 2000s, the standard outfit for crowd control had changed dramatically. It was not unusual for police at major protests to wear Kevlar helmets, full visors, chest protectors, hard shell shin guards, and heavy boots. Many carried truncheons and polycarbonate shields, and a supply of nylon disposable handcuffs to restrain protesters quickly. Today we know what to call this equipment: riot gear. That phrase was unknown in the United States and Britain before the 1970s. It became a commonly used term in Britain the early years of the Thatcher government and more familiar in the United States throughout the 1990s and 2000s.

Police forces also acquired "nonlethal" technologies to intimidate and disperse crowds. British police first launched CS gas canisters against rioters in 1981. CS gas proved less dangerous than other kinds of tear gas or vomiting gas and quickly became a familiar element of public order policing around the world. Pyrotechnic grenades were used to confuse crowds with a loud bang and dazzling light. In more extreme circumstances, police fired plastic bullets or bean-bag rounds to incapacitate dangerous elements of a mob. At the G20 summit in Pittsburgh in 2009, police experimented with sonic cannons, which disabled protesters with focused bursts of pain-inducing sound.

The arsenals of major police forces in the United States and United Kingdom became so well-stocked in the neoliberal age that some critics complained the police were being transformed into paramilitary services. Police forces also followed the military model as they improved their capacity to maintain centralized command over personnel who were deployed to contain large crowds. Written procedures for handling crowds became more detailed, special training was increased, and communications systems were upgraded. At the same time, police forces developed better procedures for obtaining help from neighboring municipalities when they were at risk of being overwhelmed. The British government established a National Reporting Center to improve the coordination of responses to severe unrest in 1984. In the United States, the federal government's role in orchestrating security for major events was formalized in a 1997 directive issued by the Clinton administration, and then by federal law in 2000.

We can see that the neoliberal age, like the first liberal age, produced substantial changes in policing capacity in both the United Kingdom and the United States. Police forces were bigger and better equipped, and more sophisticated about the use of force. A more coherent doctrine of "public order policing" emerged. (That phrase gained currency after the 1980s.) As in the first liberal age, a central theme within this doctrine was the control of territory for the purpose of preventing disruption.[158] One common tactic was relocating contentious events to remote locations. After the debacle in Seattle in 1999, the WTO held its next meeting in Qatar, a small authoritarian state in the Persian Gulf. In 2004, the United States chose to host the G8 summit on a privately owned island on the coast of Georgia. In 2010, Canada held the meeting of G7 finance ministers in a distant Arctic settlement. The 2012 G8 summit was originally planned for Chicago but later moved to the presidential retreat at Camp David, Maryland.

If meetings could not be moved to remote locations, a second-best solution was to create a de facto island within a city itself. Authorities in Quebec City prepared for a 2001 summit on free trade by surrounding the city center with a security fence that was more than two miles long. Italian officials used a similar barrier to isolate Genoa's center during the G8 meeting later in 2001. For the 2007 G8 summit, the German government surrounded the seaside resort of Heiligendamm with seven miles of fencing, eight feet tall and topped with barbed wire. For the 2009 G20 summit, Pittsburgh's central business district was also enclosed by metal fences—and by some estimates, guarded by more police than there were protesters.

As in the first liberal age, the control of public space was made easier by changes in law. In 1986, the British government adopted a new Public Order Act that expanded police authority to impose restrictions on gatherings and marches if they seemed likely to cause serious disruption. In the United States, meanwhile, city governments used their existing authority to regulate the time, place, and manner of protests more aggressively. For example, the city of Miami anticipated a 2003 free trade summit by tightening its municipal ordinance on marches and gatherings to prevent a repeat of Seattle's troubles. Similarly, the city of Chicago prepared for the 2012 NATO and G8 meetings by making municipal regulations on protests more restrictive and increasing penalties for violations. American cities often attempted to confine protests to "demonstration zones" that were isolated and easily policed. A federal judge described the demonstration zone that was created for the 2004 Democratic National Convention in Boston:

> The overall impression created by the DZ [Demonstration Zone] is that of an internment camp.... The city has chosen ... a place that was recently a construction site, not just on the wrong side of the tracks but literally under them. Between the overhead tracks, which provide very low clearance in many parts, and the multiple layers of fencing, mesh and netting, the DZ conveys the symbolic sense of a holding pen where potentially dangerous persons are separated from others.[159]

Police forces invented other techniques for containing protests. One of the most controversial methods, known as kettling, involved the use of concentrated police power to corral protesters into a secure area, where they could be held for hours and then gradually released in small numbers. The technique was devised in Germany in the late 1980s and imported into Britain and the

United States in the mid-1990s. A police official in New York City told the criminologist Luis Fernandez how the technique was applied during protests at the World Economic Forum in 2002:

> We had a system of barricaded streets that we built. This is a system where we put people in pens, metal barricades. We make these large boxed-in areas where we know people are going to end up. We design breaks so that not everyone is in the same place . . . We do this systematic enough that we can control the crowd. We build one, fill it with people, section it off, and then we build another, and so on, until the entire crowd is contained in neat boxes.[160]

Kettling was used during at the G20 summit in London in 2009. Four thousand protesters were held for seven hours in an attempt to prevent "disruption and disorder" from spreading throughout the city's financial district.[161] The containment continued until major financial institutions had closed for the day. "The police managed the crowd by keeping them penned in like sheep," one demonstrator complained.[162]

Police forces also intensified surveillance of protest activities. In 1999, the British government established a national police unit to gather intelligence on protests that threatened violence and disruption. After the 2003 free trade summit, Miami Police described how they had monitored protesters:

> Confidential surveillance grids were devised to keep tabs on developing threats during demonstrations and marches. The intelligence component established a confidential number of permanent fixed grids around the downtown area. . . . Officers in undercover roles were assigned to the grids. . . . The function of each grid officer was to monitor the area for any radical group activities and to file an immediate report to the Operations Center by phone or radio while still maintaining their undercover role.[163]

Surveillance was made easier by the increased use of closed-circuit television (CCTV) to monitor public spaces. In 2011 it was estimated that there were almost 2 million CCTV cameras watching public spaces in Britain, and perhaps 30 million in the United States. After the 2011 London riots, police gathered so much footage from CCTV cameras that it would have taken one individual more than seventeen years to watch it all. The processing of CCTV footage was simplified by computerized facial recognition technologies—but these technologies only worked if faces were visible to surveillance cameras. After the 2011 riots, the British government quickly proposed a new law to limit the wearing of masks by protesters. Pittsburgh's mayor also proposed an antimask ordinance during preparations for the 2009 G20 summit. New York City police revived a nineteenth-century antimask law during the Occupy protests in 2011.

Many of these changes in police capacities and tactics were a direct response to changes in the character of unrest in the neoliberal age. As major unions declined in influence, so too did forms of mass protest that had a certain kind of internal structure and self-discipline. New kinds of unrest—such the nonhierarchical, network-based forms of protest that were celebrated after Seattle—came to the foreground. As the sociologist P.A.J. Waddington suggested, these were more fluid forms of disruption in which a mass of people lacked clear leadership and either the capacity or will to impose order on itself. Police forces compensated for this change by developing new techniques that imposed discipline on the crowd.[164]

Politicians and security officials justified the ratcheting up of discipline by reminding the public of the danger of the uncontrolled crowd. That is to say, they refined the language of crowd control, just as they had in the first liberal age. The specter of

Seattle was raised over every subsequent economic summit, and major media, attracted by stories of potential conflict, helped to stoke public anxieties. A civilian panel appointed to investigate the handling of protests at the free trade summit in Miami in 2003 observed:

> For several months preceding the [summit], the local media devoted considerable coverage to violent protests and wanton vandalism that had taken place in other locations where international economic conferences were held.... Repeated television images of violent protests at such events contributed to an apprehension that similar chaos and violence would befall the City of Miami.[165]

Increasingly, protesters complained that they were routinely treated by police as potential adversaries. An independent report on the G20 summit in Toronto in 2010 observed that "police were seen [by protesters] to be treating all demonstrators as threats to public safety. For the most part, this was accurate.... [One senior police officer] continually referred to crowds as 'protesters/terrorists.'"[166] An important effect of new policing tactics, another study concluded, was to convey the messages that protests are "a matter of violence, aggression, and imminent general danger."[167]

Technocratic Crisis Management

The Anglo-American strategy for dealing with economic unrest did not rely entirely on the repression of protest. A final part of the story had to do with the prevention of disorder through the overall management of the economy. Here, again, the path followed by the American and British governments was pragmatic, and it was not fully revealed until the crisis that began in 2008. During that crisis, neither government stuck to the strict neoliberal line on fiscal and economic policy. Both engaged in experimentation to avoid economic collapse—with the caveat that experiments were kept in the hands of technocrats, not politicians. The effect of the crisis was to produce an unprecedented model of technocratic crisis management.

The predicament for policymakers in many countries immediately after 2008 was that neoliberal doctrine offered little by way of relief in the face of economic collapse. Before 1975 it was settled wisdom that governments should help a declining economy through an increase in government spending. Alternately, governments could use their power over central banks to lower interest rates, which would also stimulate the economy. But neoliberals were skeptical about the wisdom of allowing politicians too much discretion over fiscal and monetary policy.

On fiscal policy—that is, taxing and spending—neoliberals argued that politicians had a habit of spending too much, and taxing too little, in good times as well as bad. If politicians could not be trusted to exercise their fiscal powers responsibly, neoliberals argued, then the next-best policy was to limit their discretion with simple rules. For example, politicians can be required to balance budgets in hard times as well as good times. This eliminated the option of stimulative spending during slumps, but prevented the larger evil of debt accumulation in the long run. Neoliberals argued that this was not much a sacrifice, because the stimulative effect of deficit spending was overrated in any case. Some even claimed that strict fiscal discipline would speed an economic recovery by boosting consumer and business confidence. This was the argument for "expansionary austerity."[168]

Neoliberals had an equally dismal view about politicians' competence in managing monetary policy. Neoliberals argued that politicians found it hard to increase interest rates when the economy was doing well, which tended to produce inflation. Neo-liberals also complained that political decision making was muddled and hard to predict, which complicated long-term planning by businesses and households. The better approach, they argued, was to transfer responsibility for monetary policy to an independent central bank that was protected from political influence. Neoliberals had two replies to the objection that this was an undemocratic way of making important decisions about economic policy. The first was that central banks did not make the kind of decisions that most clearly require political guidance—that is, decisions about the distribution of wealth between one group and another. To put it colloquially, central banks did not pick winners and losers. Central banks merely influenced interest rates and the rate of inflation—and these factors, like the rain, fell equally on everyone.[169]

Neoliberals conceded that a problem of democratic accountability might arise if a central bank had discretion to choose between its goals—for example, between avoiding short-term unemployment or avoiding long-term inflation. Choosing between these two objectives might require political judgment, because it might involve putting the needs of one group (such as jobseekers) ahead of the needs of another group (such as investors). But if a bank was given only one goal, such as avoiding inflation, then the crucial political judgment was already made. The bank was left with the purely technical problem of deciding how to achieve that one goal.[170] This was alleged to be the situation of an independent central bank in the neoliberal model. It had one goal, chosen by elected officials: to maintain a low and stable rate of inflation. This was also known as the goal of price stability.

The institutional arrangements that were set up for some European countries under the Treaty on European Union in 1992 captured the neoliberal ethos perfectly. Under the treaty, countries that wanted to use the common currency, the euro, could never have an annual budget deficit exceeding 3 percent of GDP. This was not exactly a requirement for permanent budget balance, but it was still an unprecedented restriction on national finances. Countries were also prohibited from raising their total government debt higher than 60 percent of GDP. At the same time, countries in the Eurozone (as it came to be called) surrendered control over monetary policy. National central banks no longer had the power to influence interest rates. This power now belonged solely to the European Central Bank, which was run by technocrats who were carefully protected from political interference. The Treaty on European Union gave the European Central Bank a single, narrowly defined goal. As Jean-Claude Trichet, the former French bureaucrat who was head of the European Central Bank from 2003 to 2011, explained in 2008: "We have only one needle in our compass. We have to delivery price stability."[171]

In the 1990s, neoliberals regarded the treaty rules as a foundation for stable growth. After 2008, however, the treaty rules condemned many of the weaker Eurozone countries to economic stagnation. These nations had no effective tools for saving their declining economies. Previously, they might have borrowed money for stimulative spending programs. But the limits on deficits and debts that were laid out in the treaty made it difficult for them to do this. Similarly, a Eurozone country's central bank previously might have been instructed by the national government to print more money to buy its debt. This would have stimulated domestic demand by lowering interest rates; increased exports by depreciating the national currency; and reduced the government's dependence on foreign lenders to finance its deficits. But treaty rules eliminated this option as well. Only the European Central

Bank could print more money, and the treaty said that it could not do this if it seemed likely to encourage inflation in the Eurozone as a whole. The treaty also prohibited the purchase of government debt by the European Central Bank. After 2008, the bank launched some initiatives to help struggling Eurozone countries by buying their government bonds. But these programs were delayed and limited, precisely because they appeared to violate the spirit of the 1992 treaty.

The result was that weaker Eurozone economies were caught in a trap. The only path available to the governments of these nations was austerity. Government spending had to be reduced to comply with treaty requirements and produce enough surplus revenue to repay foreign creditors. This austerity did not promote economic expansion, as some neoliberals had hoped. On the contrary, it caused further economic decline. One result was a dramatic increase in the rate of youth unemployment in the weakest Eurozone economies. By 2012, it exceeded 50 percent in Greece and Spain, and 30 percent in Ireland, Italy, and Portugal. (By contrast, the youth unemployment rate was 16 percent in the United States, and 20 percent in the United Kingdom.) Neoliberal strictures sowed the seeds for continuing unrest, particularly among unemployed youth.

Ironically, the two countries that were usually regarded as the leaders of the neoliberal revolution—the United Kingdom and United States—responded more pragmatically to the risk of economic collapse. Neither country faced legal constraints on fiscal policy like those in the Treaty on European Union, and in the early months of the crisis, both tried to bolster their economies through increased government spending. The American stimulus program offered $800 billion in new spending and tax relief, roughly equally to 5 percent of U.S. GDP. (Many economists thought it should have been larger, but President Obama's advisors worried about "spooking the markets.")[172] Followers of the long-dead Keynes looked at these measures and celebrated the revival of his ideas about the importance of government spending during slumps.[173]

The celebration was premature. By 2010, both countries had veered away from stimulative fiscal policies. In the United Kingdom, a new Conservative-led coalition government promised to balance the budget through deep cuts in spending. Prime Minister David Cameron said that "urgent action" was essential to restore investor confidence in Britain.[174] In the United States, meanwhile, Congress balked at additional stimulus programs, even though the economy was still operating well below its potential. In practice, the United States also followed a path of fiscal consolidation, with the federal deficit shrinking as a share of GDP in every year of the crisis.

On fiscal policy, neoliberal doctrine eventually prevailed. This was not primarily because there was widespread faith in the doctrine of expansionary austerity. On the contrary, many people acknowledged that austerity was actually hurting national economies in the short run. What undermined the revival of Keynesian pump-priming was skepticism about the reliability of politicians in the longer run. Proper Keynesian policy required that politicians should reverse course and pay down debt when the economy improved. However, many people doubted whether American or British politicians could be trusted to do this. An alternative to relying on the good faith of politicians was to devise some way of tying their hands so that a longer-term commitment to budget balancing was "anchored and irreversible."[175] But it seemed impossible to invent rules about future spending and taxing that politicians could not circumvent. As a result, American and British governments reverted to the second-best policy preferred by neoliberals: a simple policy that required fiscal discipline in bad times as well as good times, even if that meant an increase in short-term economic pain.

By contrast, the shift on monetary policy in the United States and the United Kingdom was dramatic. Throughout the crisis, the Federal Reserve and the Bank of England engaged in unabashed experimentation as they struggled to save the two economies from collapse. In the first months of the crisis, the Federal Reserve provided massive support to struggling commercial banks. This is the classical function of a central bank during a crisis. However, the Federal Reserve went further—providing aid to financial institutions not usually protected by central banks, as well as to insurance companies, automobile financing companies, and major businesses such as Harley-Davidson, Verizon, McDonald's, and General Electric. This action was unprecedented. By January 2009, the Federal Reserve was the single most important source of short-term financing for large corporations.[176]

As the crisis continued, so did experimentation by British and American central bankers. This was made possible because the neoliberal dogma was not cemented in law, as it was in the Treaty on European Union. The United Kingdom had refused to join the Eurozone in 1992. It kept its own currency and the Bank of England retained the capacity to print more of it as circumstances required. Admittedly, the 1998 law that confirmed the independence of the Bank of England recognized price stability as its main goal, but the legal constraints on British monetary policy was not as tight as in the Treaty of European Union. Similarly, the law governing the Federal Reserve was phrased broadly. According to a 1977 law, the U.S. central bank is supposed to promote "maximum employment" as well as "stable prices." During the neoliberal heyday, the Federal Reserve had simply promoted the second goal rather than the first: Federal Reserve officials argued that the best way to promote maximum employment was by emphasizing price stability.

As the economic crisis deepened, however, both central banks moved away from their fixation on price stability. In Britain, the governor of the Bank of England was required to write an open letter if there was a significant deviation from its inflation target in the preceding three months. This was supposed to reinforce its focus on price stability. In the first decade of its independence (from 1998 to April 2007), not a single letter had to be written. But fourteen of these letters were written in the next five years, as the bank kept interest rates low to encourage growth. The bank understood that its credibility as a champion of price stability was at risk. Even so, it declined to take steps that would "risk derailing the recovery."[177] There was a similar shift in policy at the Federal Reserve. In December 2008, it promised to stimulate short-term growth by keeping interest rates at "exceptionally low" levels for the indefinite future. By 2011 this had been transformed into a commitment to maintain low rates until 2015. And in 2012, the Federal Reserve promised to keep rates down so long as the unemployment rate remained above 6.5 percent and longer-term inflation risks seemed manageable. In the short run, the Federal Reserve was ready to overshoot its inflation target to achieve a reduction in unemployment.[178] As in Britain, price stability receded in importance.

Central bankers in the United States and Britain also shifted policy in another way. In March 2009, the Federal Reserve began large-scale purchases of U.S. Treasury securities as well as the debt of two government-supported mortgage securitization enterprises, Fannie Mae and Freddie Mac. This policy became known as quantitative easing. It was specifically targeted at reducing longer-run interest rates. The federal government had a large budget deficit, and if the demand for long-term government debt was not robust, then the interest rate required by lenders was bound to increase. The Federal Reserve created that demand by buying government debt with newly created money. The Federal Reserve knew it was breaking with neoliberal orthodoxy. In 2013 the *Financial Times* observed that the practice of creating money to buy government bonds was "the ultimate taboo" in central banking.[179] It is explicitly prohibited by the Treaty on European Union. Still, the Federal Reserve—not bound by such constraints—carried on. In 2011, its purchases were equal to 60 percent of the federal government deficit, and by the end of 2012, it had purchased $2 trillion of federally guaranteed debt. The Bank of England adopted a quantitative easing policy as well. Between 2009 and 2012 it bought almost £400 billion of British government debt with newly created money. This was roughly three-quarters of the total value of debt issued by the British Treasury to finance budget deficits in the same period.

By late 2012, the Federal Reserve and Bank of England were "neck deep in extreme policy experimentation mode."[180] Central bankers in Washington and London had no previous experience in launching a policy of quantitative easing, and they understood that there were large uncertainties associated with the exercise. No one was sure that the policy would actually bolster the economy. ("These are quite unprecedented policies," Michael Woodford, a leading expert on monetary policy, told *Rolling Stone* in 2013. "They don't have any prior experience on the basis of which to judge the effects of the policies being tried.")[181] At the same time, however, there were risks if central banks did nothing: the British and American economies could slide into depression. There was comparable uncertainty about when and how the policy should be terminated. If the "exit strategy" (as it was called) was implemented too soon, the economic recovery might be squelched. But if the exit was delayed too long, there might be a resurgence of inflation, which would damage the banks' reputation as champions of price stability.

In 2012, a British cabinet minister, Vince Cable, tried to explain the predicament confronting the Bank of England and the Federal Reserve:

> Quantitative easing is a kind of new, unorthodox way of running monetary policy.... This is an experiment. We don't know where it is going to lead. So far it has almost certainly headed off a very deep depression.... But its wider consequences, whether this will lead to inflation, the wider impacts on bank lending, these are things that are only very, very imperfectly understood. But my judgment when I was first confronted with this was that it was something that we had to try, because the alternative was probably a disaster.[182]

In one sense, Cable was right: this *was* an experiment. But in another sense, Cable's statement was misleading. It implied that he had something to do with launching the experiment. He did not, and neither did any other member of a British or American cabinet. Quantitative easing was a policy launched by technocrats within two autonomous bodies, the Bank of England and the Federal Reserve, and they would decide when and how it ended.

Central bankers expressed great confidence in their own ability to manage the uncertainties surrounding the policy. Ben Bernanke reassured the public in 2012 that the Federal Reserve "has spent considerable effort planning and testing our exit strategy and will act decisively to execute it at the appropriate time."[183] In the meantime, Bernanke promised that the central bank would continue to "recalibrate" the policy "in light of incoming information."[184]

Running a policy of quantitative easing, Bernanke added later, was like driving a car. "If the incoming data support the view that the economy is able to sustain a reasonable cruising speed, we will ease the pressure on the accelerator by gradually reducing the pace of purchases."[185]

Contrast these statements with the attitude that shaped fiscal policy during the economic crisis. There could have been experiments with fiscal policy (that is, larger stimulus initiatives) as well. There were not. This is not because the uncertainties surrounding the effect of fiscal policy experiments were larger than they were with regard to monetary policy experiments. Indeed, the uncertainties surrounding quantitative easing were probably more substantial. The crucial difference was *who was conducting the experiment.* Any experiment with fiscal policy had to be put in the unreliable hands of politicians. But experiments with monetary policy could be kept under the tight control of technocrats, who were confident of their own ability to watch the dashboard, tap on the accelerator, or touch on the brake when necessary.

By 2013, the British and American governments had developed a new way of managing the overall economy during a slump. In one respect it deviated from neoliberal doctrine, because central banks were pursuing unprecedented policies. They were doing this because strict adherence to neoliberal orthodoxy would have increased the risk of economic decline and social disorder. But in another, and perhaps more important respect, this new mode of economic management affirmed neoliberal doctrine, because it put the primary responsibility for saving the economy in the hands of technocrats, rather than politicians.

The predicament confronting policymakers in Washington and London after 2008 has often been compared to the Great Depression of the 1930s. It is useful to contrast the responses to these two crises. Admittedly, there was an appetite for innovation in the 1930s as well. "The country needs bold, persistent experimentation," Franklin Roosevelt said during his presidential campaign. "Take a method and try it. If it fails, admit it frankly and try another. But above all, try something."[186] This is an apt description of Roosevelt's New Deal program. But the New Deal involved experimentation by politicians: most of the policies contained within it were devised by political appointees in the Roosevelt administration and legislators in Congress. The Federal Reserve played a secondary role in guiding the recovery. By contrast, the situation was reversed after 2008. Politicians in Washington and London tread cautiously, while central bankers experimented boldly.

This new strategy of economic management helped to keep the peace. But it also undercut the principle of democratic accountability. Remember what the arguments in defense of central bank independence had been: central bankers do not pick winners and losers; they do not choose between competing goals; they make purely instrumental decisions about how to pursue the policy of price stability. After 2008, all of this was contestable. Central bankers decided who would be thrown a lifeline, and who would not. They wrestled with the tension between promoting short-term growth and maintaining long-term price stability. And they launched experimental policies that would affect the well-being of the whole country for years to come. All of this required political as well as technical judgment. These facts might have justified an attempt to reestablish political control over the Federal Reserve and the Bank of England. But no serious attempt to restore political control was undertaken. Although there were some efforts in the United States to increase congressional influence over the Federal Reserve, none had a substantial effect on its autonomy. The overall effect of the current crisis was to affirm that the delegation of power to independent central bankers was, in fact, much broader than the public had been led to believe. The task of economic crisis management was now assigned primarily to technocrats.

The New Politics of Intolerance

So far we have described a set of laws and practices that have helped to discourage unrest in the United States and the United Kingdom during hard times. Together they constitute a formula for keeping the peace. There is one additional element that we should mention, which falls in the realm of practical politics. These laws and practices remain in place because powerful forces put pressure on governments to maintain them. The forces operating on governments were diverse, but they all contributed to an unprecedented intolerance of social and economic disruption.

Intolerance of disruption is not entirely new. Recall what Karl Polanyi said in 1944 about the decline in tolerance for unrest during the first age of liberalization: "The market system was more allergic to rioting than any other economic system we know. . . . Breaches of the peace . . . were deemed an incipient rebellion and an acute danger to the state; stocks collapsed and there was no bottom in prices."[187] Polanyi was talking about rioting, but today we can say the same about any form of unrest. International financial markets have become acutely sensitive to signs that a government is losing its grip. We are familiar with the routine: a mass demonstration in a national capital raises doubts about the capacity of a government to execute the neoliberal script. Ratings agencies warn about "slippage" and investors become skittish. To restore confidence, government leaders use police or paramilitary forces to restore order in the streets and confidence among financiers.

"Capital markets," the American financier Roger Altman said in 2013, are "the most powerful force on earth. . . . [They] can effect changes beyond the capacity of normal political processes."[188] But the pressure on governments to avoid disruption did not come from financial markets alone. The transformation of manufacturing and distribution in the neoliberal age has created other constituencies with a similar intolerance for unrest. Methods of manufacturing and selling goods changed in several ways in this era. As businesses hunted for lower production costs, the location in which goods were manufactured became more distant from the location in which they were sold. Moreover, the task of manufacturing goods was itself broken down. Increasingly, companies assembled goods using components produced at many other locations, often thousands of miles apart. Businesses were able to make these complex production chains work because of vastly expanded systems of marine, air, and land transportation. They learned how to orchestrate shipments so that the cost of maintaining large inventories was minimized.

A 2008 report from the World Economic Forum has described this transformation as the hyperoptimization of global production.[189] These changes reduced manufacturing costs and played an important part in lowering inflation in the neoliberal age. But hyperoptimization also produced a hypersensitivity about supply chain disruptions that was shared by a broad range of powerful business interests. When workers at UPS, the largest package delivery company in the United States, went on strike in 1997, the *Wall Street Journal* feared that it would "hobble everyday life in thousands of businesses and households across the country."[190] There was immediate pressure on the White House to intervene, and Labor Secretary Alexis Herman mediated a quick end to the strike. There was similar anguish within the business community in 2002, when a labor dispute closed ports that handled the United States' booming Pacific trade. Within days, President George W. Bush invoked a rarely used law to reopen the ports in the interest of "national health and safety." Shippers and retailers lobbied the Obama administration to use the same law to avoid a shutdown of East Coast ports in 2012. Even the short disruption of West Coast ports by Occupy protesters in December 2011 provoked concern within the business community. The Occupiers "managed to put a grimy paw around the neck of the U.S. economy," complained *Investor's Business Daily*. "For this costly port stunt, they should be held accountable."[191]

Economic transformation has heightened intolerance of disruption in other ways as well. We have already seen how New York City became more sensitive to its "brand image" as its economic base shifted from manufacturing to service industries such as finance, communications, and tourism. This contributed to the city's tougher response to petty street crimes that heightened the perception of disorder. Many other cities made the same adjustment. The aim of urban branding, two experts observed in 2008, was to attract visitors and investors with a vision of "the harmonious city."[192] Any disruption that threatened the perception of harmony provoked a strong reaction from business interests that had a stake in the new urban economy. This was vividly illustrated when London was threatened with unrest during the current economic crisis. Shortly after anti-austerity protests in early 2011, a British newspaper warned London's police that they should "make sure they don't lose control of London again. . . . With Britain's economy on its knees, we need every boost we can get."[193] Civic leaders wanted to protect the tourist influx that was expected because of the royal wedding in April 2011. There was more frustration among business leaders when rioting hit parts of London a few months later. British retailers worried that it sent "an ap-palling message to would-be tourists."[194] An association of public relations consultants reported that most of its members expected the riots to have a significant impact on London's international reputation. "The riots have been a PR disaster," the association's head concluded.[195]

It is not just business leaders who have shown a heightened in-tolerance of disruption. In both the United States and the United Kingdom, there has been widespread public support for tougher policing, whether it is targeted toward crime or control of pro-tests. A survey conducted after the 2009 G20 summit in London found that "the majority of the public has limited tolerance for disruption caused by protest."[196] At the same time, most people said that they had a "high level of tolerance" for police tactics such as kettling if they would avoid the interruption of their daily rou-tines. Similar attitudes may have contributed to the collapse of public support for the Occupy protests in the United States, even among Americans who said they supported the protesters' goals. Occupy Wall Street slipped from the status of novelty to public nuisance, even though the Occupy camps had a negligible effect on everyday routines in major American cities.

This intensified public intolerance of disruption may have roots in the new structure of the global economy. Public support for tougher policing was accompanied by the perception in both the United States and the United Kingdom that disorder was steadily rising. This perception was at odds with the available data, which showed a decline in rates of crime against persons and property. "Increases in fear of crime and perceived levels of crime," a 2010 study for the U.S. Department of Justice concluded, "are not con-sistent with the national trend in crime as measured by either personal victimization or reported crime."[197] This disconnection between perception and evidence was relatively new. Before the 1980s, there was a closer relationship between public attitudes and official crime statistics.

Economic transformation may help to explain why the fear of crime has become unmoored from the realities of disorder since the 1980s. Criminologists argue that the fear of crime now reflects "a diffuse anxiety about risk, rather than any pattern of everyday concerns over personal safety."[198] Research in Britain has shown that this "diffuse anxiety" is aggravated by declining economic security. And as the Jacob Hacker has observed, it is undoubtedly the case that perceptions of economic security among Americans have declined sharply over the last quarter-century. Even as the post-1980 economy experienced robust growth, Americans expressed mounting concerns about losing their jobs, coping with family emergencies, and planning for retirement.[199] Of course, there is an irony at work here. It is precisely these kinds of worries that we might expect would fuel public unrest. But if there is no effective mechanism for mobilizing that discontent, we can imagine how it might have the contrary effect of heightening intolerance for disruption. Like financiers and other businessmen, families living on the edge might have a stronger appetite for policies that offer security instead.

5

The End of Crowd Politics

"Why don't Americans protest when they're pissed?" That is what one U.S. writer asked in 2011. That is also what Joseph Schumpeter or Karl Polanyi, recollecting the history of the United States and Britain in the first liberal age, might have wondered if they were alive today. And that is what the leaders of many governments in the developing world, wrestling with effects of their own experiments with free-market reforms, might have asked as well. The bulk of our experience tells us that unrest is an intrinsic part of the free-market model. But not in the United States today, even during the worst economic crisis in a generation.

The country remained at peace because it—along with the United Kingdom, the other national leader of the free-market revolution—took steps that were not included in the neat blueprints for free-market reform that were exported to other countries. American and British politicians pursued policies that undercut the social infrastructure that is necessary to transform discontent into mass action. They ignored strictures about downsizing government and increased their investment in public order policing. They developed new methods of technocratic crisis management that reconciled the neoliberal disdain for democratic politics with the immediate need to avert total economic collapse. The *complete* formula for market reform, as it was executed in Britain and the United States, was therefore more extensive and pragmatic than many people might have realized. And it worked, in the sense that it has avoided significant unrest and disruption of trade and commerce.

One of the consequences that flowed from the implementation of this formula was the near-extinction of crowds as important players in national politics. In 1900, the sociologist Gustav Le Bon predicted that the coming century would be the "era of crowds."[200] It was a plausible hypothesis at the time. In the nineteenth century, everyday politics was routinely shaped by the mass action of citizens—in the form of strikes, demonstrations, marches, and riots. But it would be difficult to argue in 2013 that crowds still exercise political power in the same way. Certainly, we still have the experience of being in very large crowds. The number of people who gathered in the New Orleans Superdome to watch Super Bowl XLVIII in 2013 exceeded the total population of Boston in 1830, and the average attendance at a Bruce Springsteen concert in 2012 exceeded the population of Chicago in 1850. But these were not angry and politicized crowds, frustrated by economic distress and gathered for the purpose of obtaining a change in government policy. On the contrary, they were domesticated crowds that were carefully shepherded for the purposes of entertainment and commerce. The angry crowd, by contrast, was rarer and more tightly policed. It was becoming extinct because crowds wield influence through disruption, and the neoliberal age made us more allergic to disruption than ever before.

Should we care about the demise of crowd politics as a mode of political action? There is an argument that it is simply an anachronism—the relic of an earlier time, when democratic politics was not yet fully developed. In the nineteenth century most adults in the United States and United Kingdom could not vote. There was no such thing as opinion polling, and the capacity of politicians to gauge the public mood was limited. At that time, we could argue, unrest performed two important functions. It served as a safety valve that allowed people to release their frustration during hard times, and it provided a signal to politicians that action was necessary to prevent more serious forms of disorder. Today, on the other hand, we live in a world where more people can vote, politicians are more sensitive to opinion, and the rough methods of crowd politics are unnecessary.

At least, that is the argument. It makes strong assumptions about the effectiveness of the democratic institutions in giving expression to public frustrations about the economy. In fact, one of the aims of protesters since the financial crisis has been to point out the ways in which the democratic process has itself been undermined during the neoliberal age. The Occupy protesters were not alone in believing that the moneyed interests who thrived because of free-market policies had also succeeded in capturing the attention of Congress and the executive branch of the U.S. government. In 2009, Simon Johnson—a distinguished economist and one-time advisor to the International Monetary Fund—called the United States the world's "most advanced oligarchy."[201]

The problem was not just that democratic institutions had been captured by well-heeled interests. There was a larger hypocrisy at work when advocates of free-market policies said that citizens had a remedy for their grievances through traditional democratic processes. After all, one of the core ideas of the neoliberal program is that democratic institutions simply do not work that well. Voters and politicians are presumed to be shortsighted, selfish, and irrational. Consequently one of the aims of the neoliberal project has been to restrict the authority of democratic institutions—by imposing controls such as those in the Treaty on European Union; by empowering technocrats (such as central bankers) who are carefully protected from political influence; and by giving international capital markets a de facto veto over government policies. In other words, the very institutions that are supposed to function as the vehicle for responding to public discontent have been hobbled so that they cannot do this properly.

Before the crash of 2008, many people thought that the neoliberal age had produced a political and economic order that was remarkably durable. This sort of thinking went far beyond the claim that the cycle of boom and slump that had typified the first liberal age had been conquered. The proposition was that the "market-centered order" had to survive because there was no rival ideology that offered an appealing way of organizing social and economic life. As Margaret Thatcher famously put it, there was no alternative to economic liberalism. This sort of thinking tended to assume that any threat to the market-centered order must arise from outside the order itself, perhaps from another group of nations that organized themselves on different principles. It neglected what Schumpeter and Polanyi saw so clearly: the *inherent* threat to the persistence of the market system. The natural tendency of a loosely regulated market economy, experience told them, was to create discontent which may be so severe that the system itself collapses. Governments had to find ways of dealing with this risk, by deterring or managing the unrest that invariably arose when market forces were unleashed.

In the last three decades, the two countries that led the free-market revolution—the United States and Britain—have found one way of dealing with the tensions inherent in the globalized free-market system. Their formula includes measures designed to limit popular mobilization of discontent, enable the quick containment of unrest, and give primary responsibility for economic crisis management to technocrats. This is not a doctrinally elegant combination of policies, but for the moment it works. It has allowed a globalized free-market economy to continue functioning. How long it will continue to work is a different question.

Notes

1. Paul Mason, "Twenty Reasons Why It's Kicking Off Everywhere," *BBC Newsnight*, February 5, 2011. Available at http://www.bbc.co.uk/blogs/newsnight/paulmason/2011/02/twenty_reasons_why_its_kicking.html.

2. Eileen Smith, "Why Don't Americans Protest When They're Pissed?" *Matador Network.com*, September 9, 2011. Available at http://matadornetwork.com/change/why-dont-americans-protest-when-theyre-pissed/.

3. John Cunniff, "The Big Recession," Associated Press, December 27, 1982.

4. Kari Lydersen, *Revolt on Goose Island: The Chicago Factory Takeover and What It Says About the Economic Crisis* (Brooklyn, NY: Melville House, 2009), 159–60.

5. National Association of State Budget Officers, *Fiscal Survey of States December 2009* (Washington, DC: National Association of State Budget Officers, 2009), vii.

6. Sarah van Gelder, ed., *This Changes Everything* (San Francisco: Berrett-Koehler, 2011), 74.

7. Janet Byrne, ed., *The Occupy Handbook*, Kindle ed. (New York: Little, Brown, 2012), 468.

8. Writers for the 99%, ed., *Occupying Wall Street: The Inside Story of an Action That Changed America*, Kindle ed. (New York: O/R Books, 2012), Location 58.

9. Joe Nocera, "Two Days in September," *New York Times*, September 14, 2012, 23. Available at http://www.nytimes.com/2012/09/15/opinion/nocera-two-days-in-september.html?smid=pl-share.

10. Sam Pizzigati, "Why Aren't More of Us Protesting Inequality?" *Inequality.org*, March 17, 2013. Available at http://inequality.org/protesting-inequality/

11. Joseph Alois Schumpeter, *Capitalism, Socialism, and Democracy*, 5th ed. (London: Allen and Unwin, 1976), 77 and 83.

12. "On the Eve of Destruction?" *Fast Company*, April 30, 2001. Available at http://www.fastcompany.com/64106/eve-destruction.

13. Joseph A. Schumpeter, *Business Cycles: A Theoretical, Historical, and Statistical Analysis of the Capitalist Process* (New York: McGraw-Hill, 1939), 102; Schumpeter, *Capitalism, Socialism, and Democracy*, 143 and 153.

14. Karl Marx and Friedrich Engels, *Manifesto of the Communist Party* (Chicago: Charles H. Kerr, 1906), 16.

15. W. Thom DeCourcy, *A Brief History of Panics and Their Periodical Occurrence in the United States* (New York: G. P. Putnam's Sons, 1893), 22–23.

16. *Everybody's Magazine*, 10, no. 2 (February 1904): 278.

17. Horace Greeley, *The Crystal Palace and Its Lessons* (New York: Dewitt and Davenport, 1851), 16.

18. Benjamin Love, *The Handbook of Manchester* (Manchester, UK: Love and Barton, 1842).

19. *Times of London*, May 28, 1808, 4.

20. *Cobbett's Weekly Political Register*, September 7, 1816, 693.

21. Charles Reith, *British Police and the Democratic Ideal* (London: Oxford University Press, 1943), 72.

22. Carl J. Griffin, "The Violent Captain Swing?" *Past and Present* 209 (2010): 149–80, 165.

23. A. C. Benson and Viscount Esher, eds., *Letters of Queen Victoria* (London: John Murray, 1908), 1.425.

24. F. C. Mather, *Public Order in the Age of the Chartists* (Manchester, UK: Manchester University Press, 1959), 160.

25. Mark Hovell, *The Chartist Movement* (London: Longmans, Green, 1918), 290.

26. Joel T. Headley, *Pen and Pencil Sketches of Great Riots* (New York: E. B. Treat, 1877), 350.

27. James F. Rhodes, *History of the United States from the Compromise of 1850* (New York: Harper and Brothers, 1893), 28.

28. Headley, *Pen and Pencil Sketches of Great Riots*, 362.

29. Edward W. Martin, *History of the Great Riots* (Dayton, OH: National Publishing, 1877), 387–91.

30. *Springfield* (MA) *Republican*, July 6, 1894, 5.

31. Commission on Industrial Relations, *Final Report* (Washington, DC: Government Printing Office, 1916), 29–30.

32. Associated Press, "Rioting Marks Red Thursday in U.S. Cities," *Tampa Morning Tribune*, March 7, 1930, 1.

33. "Police Fight Reds As Hoover Speaks," *New York Times*, October 3, 1930, 22.

34. Walker S. Burl, "Bonus Army Is In Full Retreat; Camps Burned; Troops Use Gas," *Cleveland Plain Dealer*, July 29, 1932, 1.

35. Joseph Schumpeter, "The Instability of Capitalism," *Economic Journal* 38, no. 151 (1928): 361–86, 362.

36. Joseph A. Schumpeter and Richard Swedberg, *The Economics and Sociology of Capitalism* (Princeton, NJ: Princeton University Press, 1991), 298 and 305–6.

37. Frances Fox Piven and Richard A. Cloward, *Poor People's Movements: Why They Succeed, How They Fail* (New York: Vintage Books, 1979), 27.

38. Edward Thompson, "The Moral Economy of the English Crowd in the Eighteenth Century," *Past and Present* 50, no. 1 (1971): 122.

39. Paul A. Gilje, *The Road to Mobocracy: Popular Disorder in New York City, 1763–1834* (Chapel Hill: University of North Carolina Press, 1987), 5.

40. Pauline Maier, "Popular Uprisings and Civil Authority in Eighteenth-Century America," *William and Mary Quarterly* 27, no. 1 (1970): 4–35, 24.

41. Karl Polanyi, *The Great Transformation* (Boston: Beacon Press, 2001), 195–96.

42. *The Nation*, August 9, 1877, 85.

43. James McCabe, *The History of the Great Riots* (Philadelphia: National Publishing, 1877), 3.

44. David G. Chandler and I.F.W. Beckett, *The Oxford History of the British Army* (New York: Oxford University Press, 2003), 162.

45. Reith, *British Police and the Democratic Ideal*, 9; Charles Tilly, *Popular Contention in Great Britain, 1758–1834* (Boulder, CO: Paradigm, 2005), 23.

46. *Annual Register*, 1823, 84.

47. Charles Reith, *The Police Idea: Its History and Evolution in England in the Eighteenth Century and After* (London: Oxford University Press, 1938), 253.

48. Reith, *British Police and the Democratic Ideal*, 72–73.

49. *Hazard's Register of Pennsylvania* 9 (January–July 1832): 218.

50. Alasdair Roberts, *America's First Great Depression: Economic Crisis and Political Disorder after the Panic of 1837* (Ithaca, NY: Cornell University Press, 2012), 171.

51. Edward K. Spann, *New Metropolis: New York City, 1840–1857* (New York: Columbia University Press, 1981), 317.

52. Peleg W. Chandler, "The Spirit of Misrule," *Law Reporter* 7 (1844): 209–21, 220.

53. *The Nation*, August 9, 1877, 85.

54. *Report of the Secretary of War* (Washington, DC: Government Printing Office, 1877).

55. "Our National Guard," *New York Herald*, August 5, 1877, 8.

56. Jerry M. Cooper, *The Rise of the National Guard: The Evolution of the American Militia, 1865–1920* (Lincoln: University of Nebraska Press, 1997), 30.

57. War Department, *The Organized Militia of the United States in 1895* (Washington, DC: Government Printing Office, 1896), 22, 152, 184.

58. "Practicing The Riot Drill," *New Haven Register*, May 6, 1886, 1.

59. Winthrop Alexander, "Ten Years of Riot Duty," *Journal of the Military Service Institution of the United States* 19 (1896): 26 and 62.

60. Joel P. Bishop, *Commentaries on the Criminal Law*, 6th ed. (Boston: Little, Brown, 1877), 2.125.

61. Albert V. Dicey, *Introduction to the Study of the Law of the Constitution*, 8th ed. (London: Macmillan, 1915), 267.

62. *Davis v. Massachusetts* 167 US 43 (1897).

63. *Hague v. CIO* 307 US 496 (1939).

64. David Pinckney, "Napoleon III's Transformation of Paris: The Origins and Development of the Idea," *Journal of Modern History* 27, no. 2 (1955): 125–34, 132.

65. William Cobbett, *The Parliamentary History of England* (London: T. C. Hansard, 1817), 30:495.

66. Dana Arnold, "Rationality, Safety, and Power: The Street Planning of Later Georgian London," *Georgian Group Journal* (1995): 37–50, 50.

67. *Journal of the Military Service Institution of the United States* 4 (1883): 364.

68. Robert M. Fogelson, *America's Armories: Architecture, Society, and Public Order* (Cambridge, MA: Harvard University Press, 1989), 131–33.

69. Boston Landmarks Commission, *Study Report on the Armory of the First Corps of Cadets* (Boston: Boston Landmarks Commission, 1977).

70. Joseph E. Gary, "The Enforcement of the Law," *Public Policy* 9, no. 24 (December 12, 1903): 286.

71. Ruth McKenney, *Industrial Valley* (New York: Harcourt, 1939), 360.

72. "The Chicago Anarchists of 1886," *The Century Magazine* 45, no. 6 (April 1893): 810.

73. Advertisement by the Henningsen Agency, *New Ulm Review*, March 24, 1920, 8.

74. Albert Ordway, *The National Guard in Service* (Washington, DC: J. J. Chapman, 1891), 307.

75. United States Strike Commission, *Report on the Chicago Strike* (Washington, DC: Government Printing Office, 1895), xlv–xlvi.

76. Thomas Carlyle, *The French Revolution: A History* (London: Chapman and Hall, 1837), 1.242.

77. Charles Mackay, *Memoirs of Extraordinary Popular Delusions* (London: R. Bentley, 1841), 1.viii.

78. "Factory Question," *London Courier*, January 8, 1842, 1.

79. "Review of Literature," *Court Gazette*, April 2, 1842, 1068.

80. Charles Mackay, *Forty Years' Recollections of Life, Literature, and Public Affairs: From 1830 to 1870*, 2 vols. (London: Chapman and Hall, 1877), 2.50.

81. Hippolyte Taine, *The French Revolution* (New York: H. Holt, 1878), 1.50.

82. Gabriel Tarde, *Penal Philosophy* (Boston: Little, Brown, 1912), 50.

83. Boris Sidis, *The Psychology of Suggestion* (New York: Appleton, 1898), 17.

84. Gustave Le Bon, *The Crowd: A Study of the Popular Mind*, 2d ed. (New York: Macmillan, 1897), 16.

85. J. J. W., "Emotionalism," *New Orleans Times Picayune*, March 14, 1909, 32.

86. William Munro, "Review of 'Crisis Government, '" *A merican Political Science Review* 28, no. 4 (1934): 688–89, 688.

87. Polanyi, *The Great Transformation*, 151.

88. Herbert Spencer, *The Man versus the State* (London: Williams and Norgate, 1894), 28–31.

89. Warren G. Harding, *Inaugural Address*, March 4, 1921.

90. Polanyi, *The Great Transformation*, 251.

91. Sir William Beveridge, *Social Insurance and Allied Services* (London: His Majesty's Stationery Office, 1942), 8–9.

92. National Resources Planning Board, *National Resources Development Report for 1943* (Washington, DC: Government Printing Office, 1943), ii.

93. Democratic Party Platform, June 27, 1932. Available at http://www.presidency.ucsb.edu/ws/index.php?pid=29595.

94. B. F. Haley, "The Federal Budget: Economic Consequences of Deficit Financing," *American Economic Review* 30, no. 5 (1941): 67–87, 67.

95. Tracy Roof, *American Labor, Congress, and the Welfare State, 1935–2010*, Kindle ed. (Baltimore: Johns Hopkins University Press, 2011), Location 1756.

96. Don Woodman, "Thousands Receive Top Grange Degree in 2d Day of National Conclave Here," *Portland Oregonian*, November 15, 1946, 20.

97. "We Are All Keynesians Now," *Time*, December 31, 1965, 74.

98. Jacob S. Hacker, *The Great Risk Shift* (New York: Oxford University Press, 2006), 40.

99. Michael Mandelbaum, *The Ideas That Conquered the World: Peace, Democracy, and Free Markets in the Twenty-First Century* (New York: Public Affairs, 2002).

100. John Williamson, "What Washington Means by Policy Reform," in *Latin American Adjustment: How Much Has Happened?* ed. John Williamson (Washington, DC: Institute for International Economics, 1990), 5–20, 18.

101. Steven Weber, "The End of the Business Cycle?" *Foreign Affairs* 76, no. 4 (1997): 65–82, 65.

102. Federal Reserve Board, "Remarks by Chairman Alan Greenspan on Economic Volatility," Jackson Hole, WY, August 30, 2002.

103. William C. Dudley and R. Glenn Hubbard, *How Capital Markets Enhance Economic Performance and Facilitate Job Creation* (New York: Goldman Sachs, 2004), 3.

104. Adair Turner, *Economics after the Crisis: Objectives and Means* (Cambridge, MA: MIT Press, 2012), xii.

105. *El Caracazo Case*, Judgment of November 11, 1999, Inter-Am. Ct. H.R. (Ser. C) No. 58 (1999).

106. International Federation for Human Rights, *Observatory for the Protection of Human Rights Defenders Annual Report 2005—Guatemala*, March 22, 2006. Available at http://www.unhcr.org/refworld/docid/48747cb885.html.

107. Yu Yongding quoted in Wang Zhengyi, "Conceptualizing Economic Security and Governance: China Confronts Globalization," *Pacific Review* 17, no. 4 (2004): 523–45, 527.

108. Ma Tianjie, "Environmental Mass Incidents in Rural China," *Woodrow Wilson Center China Environmental Series* 10 (2009): 33–56, 34.

109. Robert Marquand, "In China, Stresses Spill Over Into Riots," *Christian Science Monitor*, November 22, 2004. Available at http://www.csmonitor.com/2004/1122/p01s03-woap.html.

110. Anthony DePalma, "Mexico's Rescue Package: The Overview," *York Times*, January 4, 1995, A1.

111. Paul Krugman, "Saving Asia," *Fortune*, September 7, 2008, 74–80.

112. "Moody's Lowers Argentine Ratings to Caa1," Moody's Investors Service, July 26, 2001.

113. Anthony Faiola, "State of Siege in Argentina," *Washington Post*, December 20, 2001, A1.

114. International Monetary Fund, *The IMF and Argentina, 1991–2001* (Washington, DC: International Monetary Fund, 2004), 14; Michael Mussa, *Argentina and the Fund: From Triumph to Tragedy* (Washington, DC: Institute for International Economics, 2002), 52.

115. Ben Bernanke, *The Federal Reserve and the Financial Crisis* (Princeton, NJ: Princeton University Press, 2013), 121.

116. Menzie David Chinn and Jeffry A. Frieden, *Lost Decades: The Making of America's Debt Crisis and the Long Recovery* (New York: W. W. Norton, 2011), 38.

117. IMF Survey, "Unregulated Financial Systems Make Unstable Economies," *IMF Survey Magazine*, June 20, 2012. Available at: http://www.imf.org/external/pubs/ft/survey/so/2012/int062012a.htm.

118. *Baltic News Service*, January 16, 19 and 26, 2009.

119. International Monetary Fund, *Concluding Statement on the 2009 Article IV Consultation*, June 22, 2009.

120. Edward Cody, "Unions Protest Actions on Economy," *Washington Post*, January 30, 2009, A8.

121. Philip Pangolos, "Bank Workers Killed in Riots," *The Times* (UK), May 6, 2010, 14.

122. Alan Travis, "You Can Make Savings, May Tells Police," *The Guardian*, September 16, 2010, 18. Available at http://www.guardian.co.uk/uk/2010/sep/15/theresa-may-cut-police-budget-without-violent-unrest.

123. "Met Police Commissioner Predicts 'Disorder' on Streets." Available at http://www.bbc.co.uk/news/uk-11839386, November 25, 2010.

124. Laurie Penny, "Where Are the Activists as Austerity Bites?" *The Guardian*, April 4, 2013, 34. Available at http://www.guardian.co.uk/commentisfree/2013/apr/04/where-are-the-activists-austerity.

125. Polanyi, *The Great Transformation*, 152.

126. Kari Lydersen and James Tracy, "The Real Audacity of Hope," *Dollars and Sense*, December 12, 2008. Available at http://www.dollarsandsense.org/archives/2008/1208lydersentracy.html.

127. Lydersen, *Revolt on Goose Island*, 13.

128. Chris Rhomberg, "The Return of Judicial Repression," *The Forum* 10, no. 1 (2012): 1–18, 1.

129. Peter L. Francia, *The Future of Organized Labor in American Politics*, Kindle ed. (New York: Columbia University Press, 2006).

130. A. H. Raskin, "The Air Strike Is Ominous for Labor," *New York Times*, August 16, 1981, 3:1.

131. David Shribman, "A Potpourri of Protesters," *New York Times*, September 20, 1981, 1.

132. Julia Malone, "Solidarity Day in Washington Gives Reagan Foes a Lift," *Christian Science Monitor*, September 21, 1981, 3.

133. National Association of State Budget Officers, *Fiscal Survey of States December 2009*, 41 and 43.

134. John Nichols, "Jesse Jackson tells 50,000 in Wisconsin: 'This is a Martin Luther King Moment!'" *The Nation*, February 19, 2011. Available at http://www.thenation.com/blog/158740/jesse-jackson-tells-50000-wisconsin-martin-luther-king-moment.

135. Jeffrey Jones, "Approval of Labor Unions Holds Near Its Low," *Gallup Politics*, August 31, 2011. Available at http://www.gallup.com/poll/149279/approval-labor-unions-holds-near-low.aspx.

136. Gallup Poll data on labor unions, accessed August 2013. Available at http://www.gallup.com/poll/12751/labor-unions.aspx.

137. David Graeber, *Direct Action: An Ethnography* (Oakland, CA: AK Press, 2009), 32.

138. Remarks at the National Press Club, November 19, 1999.

139. Alexander Cockburn and Jeffrey St. Clair, *Five Days That Shook the World: Seattle and Beyond* (New York: Verso, 2000), 59.

140. Naomi Klein, "Reclaiming the Commons," *New Left Review* 9 (2001): 81–89.

141. Naomi Klein, "Does Protest Need a Vision?" *The Nation*, June 22, 2000, 18–21, 19.

142. Steven Johnson, *Future Perfect: The Case for Progress in a Networked Age* (New York: Riverhead Books, 2012), 105.

143. Byrne, ed., *The Occupy Handbook*, 245.

144. Writers for the 99%, ed., *Occupying Wall Street*.

145. Byrne, ed., *The Occupy Handbook*, 122.

146. Robert McChesney, "This Isn't What Democracy Looks Like," *Monthly Review* 64, no. 6 (2012): 1–28, 19.

147. Seattle Police Department, *After Action Report on WTO Ministerial Conference* (Seattle, WA: Seattle Police Department, 2000), 3 and 5.

148. Police Executive Research Forum, *Police Management of Mass Demonstrations* (Washington, DC: Police Executive Research Forum, 2006), 1.

149. David Osborne, "Reinventing Government," *Public Productivity and Management Review* 16, no. 4 (1993): 349–56, 349.

150. Brian Reaves and Matthew Hickman, *Police Departments in Large Cities, 1990–2000* (Washington, DC: Department of Justice, Office of Justice Programs, 2002).

151. Al Baker, "When the Police Go Military," *New York Times*, December 4, 2011, 6.

152. Alex Vitale, *City of Disorder* (New York: New York University Press, 2009).

153. Eli Avraham, "Media Strategies for Improving an Unfavorable City Image," *Cities* 21, no. 6 (2004): 471–79, 472.

154. Vitale, *City of Disorder*.

155. P.A.J. Waddington, "Coercion and Accommodation: Policing Public Order after the Public Order Act," *British Journal of Sociology* 45, no. 3 (1994): 367–85, 368.

156. Helen Mills, Arianna Silvestri, and Roger Grimshaw, *Police Expenditure, 1999–2009* (London: Centre for Crime and Justice Studies, 2010), 2.

157. Edward Boyd, Rory Geoghegan, and Blair Gibbs, *Cost of the Cops: Manpower and Deployment in Policing* (London: Policy Exchange, 2011), 6–7 and 23.

158. For a more extensive discussion of this theme, see: P.A.J. Waddington, *Liberty and Order: Public Order Policing in a Capital City* (London: UCL Press, 1994), chapter 7; Don Mitchell, *The Right to the City: Social Justice and the Fight for Public Space* (New York: Guilford Press, 2003); Luis Fernandez, *Policing Dissent* (New Brunswick, NJ: Rutgers University Press, 2009); Amory Starr, Luis Fernandez, and Christian Scholl, *Shutting Down the Streets* (New York: New York University Press, 2011).

159. *Coalition to Protest the Democratic National Convention v. City of Boston*, 327 F.Supp.2d 61 (2004) at 75.

160. Fernandez, *Policing Dissent*, 132–33.

161. Her Majesty's Inspectorate of Constabulary, *Adapting to Protest* (London: Her Majesty's Inspectorate of Constabulary, July 2009), 50.

162. Financial Services Club Blog, April 1, 2009. Available at http://thefinanser.co.uk/fsclub/2009/04/london-g20-protests-update.html.

163. Miami Police Department, *FTAA after Action Review* (Miami, FL: Miami Police Department, 2004).

164. P.A.J. Waddington, *The Strong Arm of the Law: Armed and Public Order Policing* (New York: Oxford University Press, 1991), 128 and 192.

165. City of Miami Civilian Investigative Panel, *Report on the Free Trade Area of the Americas Summit* (Miami, FL: City of Miami, 2006), 11.

166. Office of the Independent Police Review Director, *Policing the Right to Protest: G20 Systemic Review Report* (Toronto, Canada: Office of the Independent Police Review Director 2012), 119.

167. Starr, Fernandez, and Scholl, *Shutting Down the Streets*, 94.

168. Mark Blyth, *Austerity: The History of a Dangerous Idea* (New York: Oxford University Press, 2010), 165.

169. Alan Blinder, "Is Government Too Political?" *Foreign Affairs* 76, no. 6 (1997): 115–26, 121.

170. Giandomenico Majone, *Regulating Europe* (New York: Routledge, 1996), 14.

171. Carter Dougherty, "In Europe, Central Banking Is Different," *New York Times*, March 6, 2008, 1.

172. Ryan Lizza, "The Obama Memos," *The New Yorker*, January 30, 2012, 36.

173. "The Keynes Comeback," *The Economist*, October 1, 2009, 94.

174. Prime Minister's speech on the economy, June 7, 2010. Available at http://www.number10.gov.uk/news/prime-ministers-speech-on-the-economy.

175. "Fiscal Policy Looks Forward," *IMF Survey Online*, April 19, 2013, Available at http://www.imf.org/external/pubs/ft/survey/so/2013/pol041913a.htm.

176. Marcin Kacperczyk and Philipp Schnabl, "When Safe Proved Risky: Commercial Paper during the Financial Crisis of 2007–2009," *Journal of Economic Perspectives* 24, no. 1 (2010): 29–50, 30.

177. Bank of England, "Overview of the Inflation Report February 2013," Available at http://www.bankofengland.co.uk/publications/Pages/inflationreport/infrep.aspx.

178. Speech by Federal Reserve Vice Chair Janet Yellen, "Revolution and Evolution in Central Bank Communications," November 13, 2012. Available at http://www.federalreserve.gov/newsevents/speech/yellen20121113a.htm.

179. Wolfgang Münchau, "Ireland Shows the Way With Its Debt Deal," *Financial Times*, February 10, 2013, Available at http://www.ft.com/cms/s/0/a4564eae-713a-11e2-9d5c-00144feab49a.html#axzz2eJnltGLO.

180. Mohamed El-Erian, "Beware the 'Central Bank Put' Bubble," *Financial Times*, October 10, 2012, Available at http://www.ft.com/intl/cms/s/0/129dba66-1121-11e2-a637-00144feabdc0.html#axzz2eJnltGLO.

181. Matt Taibbi, "The Mad Science of the National Debt," *Rolling Stone*, June 6, 2013, 48–52, 52.

182. Press Association, "Cable: QE An Unorthodox Experiment," Press Association, March 2, 2012.

183. Ben Bernanke, "Monetary Policy since the Onset of the Crisis," Speech to the Jackson Hole Symposium, August 31, 2012. Available at http://www.federalreserve.gov/newsevents/speech/bernanke20120831a.htm.

184. Ben Bernanke, *Testimony before the Joint Economic Committee* (Washington, DC: Board of Governors of the Federal Reserve System, May 22, 2013).

185. "Here's Exactly What Bernanke Said That's Driving the Global Markets Crazy," *The Business Insider*, June 21, 2013, Available at http://www.business insider.com/fomc-press-conference-transcript-june-19-2013-2013-6.

186. Address at Oglethorpe University, May 22, 1932. Available at http://newdeal.feri.org/speeches/1932d.htm.

187. Polanyi, *The Great Transformation*, 195.

188. Roger C. Altman, "The Fall and Rise of the West," *Foreign Affairs* 92, no. 1 (2013): 8–13.

189. World Economic Forum, *Global Risks 2008* (Geneva: Switzerland, 2008), 15.

190. "UPS Walkout Delivers Few Crises—So Far," *Wall Street Journal*, August 5, 1997, B1.

191. "Occupy Crowd Victimizes 99%," *Business Daily*, December 13, 2011, A14.

192. Sonya Hanna and Jennifer Rowley, "An Analysis of Terminology Use in Place Branding," *Place Branding and Public Diplomacy* 4, no. 1 (2008): 61–75, 63.

193. "Wed Card For Thugs," *Daily Star*, March 28, 2011, 6.

194. British Retail Consortium, "Rioters' Shop Attacks Condemned," August 8, 2011. Available at http://www.brc.org.uk/brc_news_detail.asp?id=2015.

195. Public Relations Consultants Association, "London Riots Damage London's Reputation," August 2011. Available at http://www.prca.org.uk/%5 CLondon_Riots_damage_Londons_reputation.

196. Her Majesty's Inspectorate of Constabulary, *Adapting to Protest*, 5.

197. Gary Cordner, *Reducing Fear of Crime* (Washington, DC: US Department of Justice, Office of Community Oriented Policing Services, 2010), 3.

198. Emily Gray, Jonathan Jackson, and Stephen Farrall, "Reassessing the Fear of Crime," *European Journal of Criminology* 5, no. 3 (2008): 363–80.

199. Hacker, *The Great Risk Shift*, 16–18. Of course, there were other considerations that contributed to a sense of diffuse anxiety during the neoliberal age. In 2011, a decade after the September 11 attacks, the Gallup Poll found that almost half of Americans were still worried about imminent terrorist attacks. The Boston terror bombings in April 2013 showed how the concern with terrorism affected attitudes about crowd control. In a Time/CNN poll conducted after the Boston bombings, 80 percent supported more extensive camera surveillance of public spaces, combined with the use of facial-recognition technology to scan for suspected terrorists within crowds.

200. Le Bon, *The Crowd*.

201. Simon Johnson, "The Quiet Coup," *The Atlantic*, May 2009, 46–56, 49. Available at http://www.theatlantic.com/magazine/archive/2009/05/the-quiet-coup/307364/.

About the Author

Alasdair Roberts is Professor of Public Affairs in the Truman School of Public Affairs at the University of Missouri. He is also a Fellow of the U.S. National Academy of Public Administration. He received his law degree from University of Toronto and his Ph.D. in Public Policy from Harvard University and is the author of several books, including *The Logic of Discipline: Global Capitalism and the New Architecture of Government; Blacked Out: Government Secrecy in the Information Age*; and from Cornell University Press, *America's First Great Depression: Economic Crisis and Political Disorder after the Panic of 1837*. His articles have appeared in *Foreign Policy, Government Executive, Foreign Affairs*, and the *Washington Post*.

CPSIA information can be obtained
at www.ICGtesting.com
Printed in the USA
LVHW101926230723
753122LV00003B/460